Monograph 18
THE AMERICAN ETHNOLOGICAL SOCIETY
Marian W. Smith, *Editor*

KWAKIUTL COPPER *(after Boas, 1897)*

HELEN CODERE

FIGHTING WITH PROPERTY

A STUDY OF KWAKIUTL POTLATCHING AND WARFARE 1792–1930

With
Tribal and Linguistic Map of Vancouver Island and Adjacent Territory
Drawn and Compiled by Vincent F. Kotschar

UNIVERSITY OF WASHINGTON PRESS
SEATTLE AND LONDON

First published 1950
Library of Congress Catalog Card Number 51-5052
Second printing, 1966
Third printing, 1970
Fourth printing, 1972
ISBN 0-295-74075-2
Printed in the United States of America

Preface

The subject of this study is the cultural history of the Kwakiutl Indians during the period from 1792 to about 1930: 1792 is the date of Vancouver's visit to the Kwakiutl, which is the first known contact of the people with Europeans; a potlatch is recorded for 1936 but data for the past twenty-five years are most inadeguate and 1930 marks a somewhat arbitrary endpoint when they give out. Within this period Kwakiutl culture was in intensive contact with the new European culture and changes occurred which were at once the development of tendencies already present in Kwakiutl life and the result of pressures put upon it by the powerful surrounding culture.

There is an exceptionally large ethnographic literature on the Kwakiutl. Franz Boas, and George Hunt under Boas' direction, recorded what is probably the largest body of textual materials that we possess for the study of any primitive culture, and in addition to this remarkable collection of work materials there are massive studies by Boas of Kwakiutl social organization, ceremonial life, mythology, art and language. Also, there exists a large amount of historical data which has never been used either in its own terms or in relation to the texts, ethnographic reports or analyses of Kwakiutl culture. It is the aim of the present study to utilize both the historical and the cultural materials in order to achieve understanding of the processes at work in Kwakiutl life under the conditions of contact.

Analysis of the historical and cultural data combined reveals a major shift to have taken place in Kwakiutl life during the time it has been known to history. This change was the great increase in the vigor of the potlatch, or the distribution of property out of rivalry for social prestige, and the co-existent decrease and final extinction of warfare and physical violence. The full proof of the occurrence of this change which the Kwakiutl themselves noted as "fighting with property" instead of "fighting with weapons" and the tracing out of the many interrelated factors that caused it to occur are the tasks of this enquiry.

The orientation of this research has been towards an understanding of the Kwakiutl as they were revealed by their history. The manifest causes of historical changes have been exhaustively examined and have required that particular prominence be given to developments in the economic field. In keeping with this approach and with the desire to present the material in the most explicit and uncontroversial way possible, little concern has been given to the "psychology" of the people. Yet it is undeniable that the results of the study, which show the Kwakiutl to have abandoned destructiveness towards life in favor of the excitement and satisfactions of a socio-economic contest, have the most profound implications not only for an understanding of the psychology of the Kwakiutl but also for a knowledge of human potentialities for change away from destructiveness, at a point in the history of the world when such a change is necessary.

The study was submitted as a dissertation in partial fulfillment of the requirements for the degree of doctor of philosophy in the Faculty of Political Science of Columbia University. To the members of my thesis committee, Ruth Benedict, Marian W. Smith, William Duncan Strong and Charles Wagley, I wish to express my deep gratitude for their encouragement and guidance in the planning and preparation of this study. To Professor B. H. Beckhart, Professor Margaret Myers and Professor Mabel Newcomer I am particularly indebted for helpful criticism concerning economic points and I am further indebted to Professor Myers for help in the use of statistical materials.

To Franz Boas any student of Kwakiutl culture owes an immeasurable debt of gratitude for the wealth of material he collected and integrated, for the clarity of his writing, and for the creativeness and rigorous documentation of his generalizations.

Helen Codere

June, 1950.
Poughkeepsie, New York

Table of Contents

ILLUSTRATIONS

TABLES

CHAPTER ONE

Introduction to Kwakiutl Life

The Kwakiutl lived upon the shores of the northern part of Vancouver Island, Canada, and the adjacent mainland. Their country is one of inlets, fjords and innumerable islands made by the depression of this region in geological times. The climate, modified by the Japan current, is relatively mild and wet, and divides into a wet season lasting from October to April, and a dryer season the rest of the year. It is a region of dense vegetation. Thick forests of giant cedar, fir and hemlock rise from a high and tangled undergrowth of vine maple, berrycane and fern. There were many land animals: mountain goat, bear and deer as well as the smaller woods animals. But for the Kwakiutl, the greatest resource of their country was to be found in its fantastically abundant sea life. There were seals, sealions, seaotters and porpoises; shellfish such as crabs, clams and mussels; many salt water fish such as halibut, cod, olachen, herring, and most important of all, the several species of salmon.

The first description of the Kwakiutl was given by Vancouver, Menzies and an unknown associate on the occasion of their visit to the territory in 1792. No systematic account of the people was begun for almost a century after that date, and knowledge about them must be assembled from the records of the Hudson's Bay Company, the reports of the Canadian government, and the early histories of British Columbia. In the 1880's Franz Boas, George Dawson and Adrian Jacobsen began the ethnographical work. Boas was to continue this work for almost half a century, and to contribute what amounts to a library of material on almost every aspect of Kwakiutl life. The most recent field work in the area was the recording of a life history by Clellan S. Ford in 1940. The ethnographic descriptions give a particularly full picture of Kwakiutl life around the turn of the century, and the summary of Kwakiutl culture which follows refers most specifically to this period. In 1900 the Kwakiutl population was about 1500, although the Kwakiutl had numbered more than twice that in the first census made in 1872, and pre-contact estimates are of a population ten times that size. Although many aspects of Kwakiutl life have now disappeared, the people themselves survive and take an active part in fishing and lumbering pursuits in their old tribal territory. A brief summary of their former culture is necessary to serve as a framework for the historic changes dealt with in this paper. But any summary of a way of life can do no more than sketch in certain broad features and suggest the wealth of detail and animation needed to make the picture complete.

Kwakiutl belongs to the Wakashan language family which comprises Kwakiutl and Nootka and is probably more closely related to the languages of the southern than to those of the northern Northwest Coast. Kwakiutl speakers included mainland groups speaking the Xa-isla and Heiltsuq dialects living in the territory of Gardiner and Douglass Channels and Rivers Inlet, as well as the groups to the south on both the mainland and the island who were ethnologically hnown as "the Kwakiutl."

The Kwakiutl were divided into about twenty-five groups which were politically autonomous to an extent which makes it meaningless to speak of the Kwakiutl "nation." The groups were, for the most part, village units although four of them lived together in a very large village at Fort Rupert, and the population decrease and other factors had made for many shifts and consolidations before the arrangement of groupings was finally recorded. The main groups referred to in the literature and in this paper may be identified by reference to the map (Fig. 1) or to the list of tribal names (Table 1). Each group or tribe of Kwakiutl was subdivided into three to seven *numayms*, a Kwakiutl word which Boas found it necessary to use for a type of bilateral lineage division not accurately described by the available terminology. The main importance of all the various orders of grouping was in the system they formed of positions of social rank. Each tribe was ranked in greatness in relation to all other tribes, and each numaym, and the individually held offices within each numaym, were similarly ranked.

TABLE 1

Kwakiutl Tribal Names[1] (Kwakiutl Dialect)

Koskimo Subdialect
1. L'ā'sq'ēnôx
2. Gua'ts'ēnôx
3. G·o'p'ēnôx
4. Qo'sqēmox (Koskimo)

Newettee Subdialect (Newettee)
1. Naqô'mg·ilisala
2. La'Lasiqoala

Kwakiutl Subdialect
1. Goasi'la
2. Nā'q'oaqtôq
3. Kwakiutl
   a. Guē'tEla
   b. Q'ō'moyuē
   c. Q'ō'mk·ūtis
   d. Wa'las Kwakiutl
4. Ma'malēleqala
5. Qoē'xsōt'ēnôx
6. Lau'itsîs
7. NE'mqîc (Nimkish)
8. T'Ena'xtax
9. A'wa-iLala
10. Ts'ā'watEēnôx
11. Guau'aēnôx
12. Haxuā'mîs
13. Lē'kwîltôq (Lekwiltok)
   a. Wī'wēqaē
   b. Xā'xamatsEs
   c. Kuē'xal
   d. Laa'luîs
   e. Q'ō'm'ēnôx

[1] Reproduced from Boas, 1897, pp. 328—331, with frequent English spellings added. Ethnographers as well as agents and travellers frequently use these

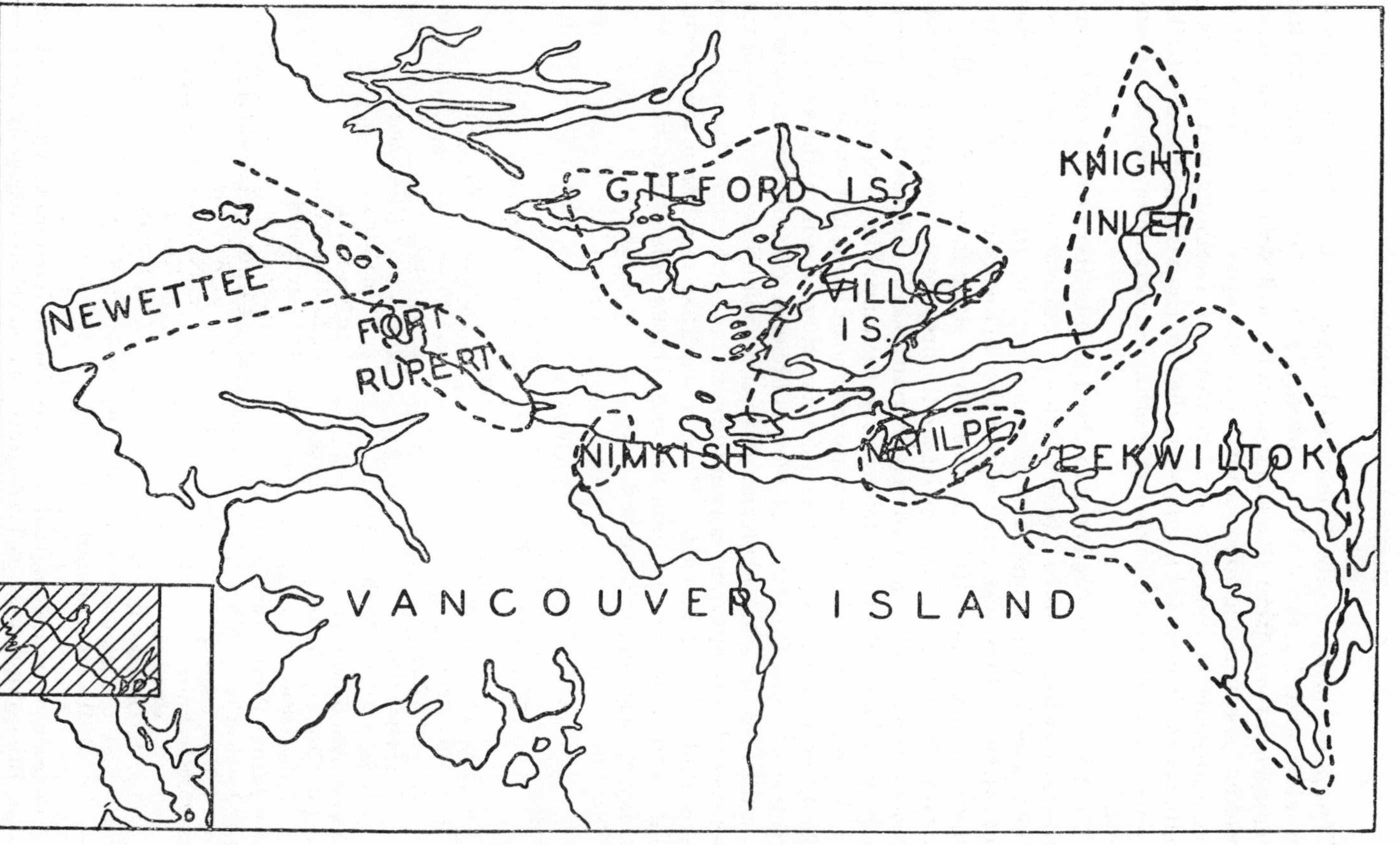

Fig. 1. Map (after Boas, 1887).

The Kwakiutl plane of living was one of the highest of any North American Indian group. They were wealthy not only in the material necessities of everyday living but also in the possession of numerous objects, tools, utensils, houses and canoes which they made as both artists and craftsmen. Although Kwakiutl wealth was closely related to the great natural wealth of the region in which they lived, it was actually produced by their magnificent technical and artistic virtuosity and by their unusual energy.

Food-getting, and particularly fishing, techniques were numerous and produced great surpluses. Highly developed storage techniques guaranteed the maximum enjoyment of these surpluses throughout the year and especially during the long winter period when the Kwakiutl stopped almost all economic activity and were preoccupied with ceremonial.

Just as they were among the best fed people of the New World, so were they among the best housed. Their multi-family houses were made of large cedar boards supported by heavy cedar posts. The house front was often painted with a large stylized representation of the mythical beings related to the family history, and the house posts were often carved. The space in the interior of the house was divided, with one great room for everyday household activities and social life and large ceremonial gatherings, and with varying numbers of private family bedrooms lining the walls on one or both sides. Paintings and carvings decorated the outside walls of the bedrooms, settees were placed in front of the bedrooms in each family's area of the house, and the wooden boxes, dishes, spoons of horn and other utensils of which they had such liberal supplies were also kept there. Women added products such as mats, blankets and baskets to the already large inventory of furnishings.

designations and in doing so they lump together the various Kwakiutl tribes speaking the same subdialect or living in the same general locality.

The Koskimo were west of the northern body of the people, neighboring the Nootka. Beginning with the Newettee, the list moves southward. The Village Island people (see Fig. 1) include the Mamalelelqala and the Kwiksotenoq; the Gilford Island group included Tsawatenoq, Kwauaenoq and Hahuamis. The Matilpe who appear on the map numbered only sixty-three in 1885 and reference to them appears as late as 1897; they probably are excluded from this list because of their inferior potlatch position according to the view of the four Fort Rupert bands listed here as "Kwakiutl". Boas made what he considered more accurate phonetic transcriptions of Kwakiutl names in later works, but since the changes from the spellings used here were not in the direction of simplification, and since the source in which the present spellings occur is frequently quoted in this study, this listing is used. Since it was necessary in this study to use such a variety of historical materials and references, it was impractical to standardize the spelling of Kwakiutl names, and it was undesirable to sacrifice precision by using the inclusive name, "Kwakiutl", in cases where the reference was to one particular tribe of Kwakiutl. The situation would not have been simplified for the reader in any case by following every Kwakiutl name in the text with Boas' close and intricate phonetic transcription.

The Kwakiutl made canoes ranging in size from those which would hold only one or two persons to the great painted canoes which would hold as many as fifty and which were used for war or for formal trips to other Kwakiutl villages for ceremonials and potlatches. These canoes were the means by which they travelled about constantly, getting their living from many fishing stations and gathering grounds, and congregating in one another's villages for ceremonials. Although the canoes were technically dugouts made from a single cedar log, the skilled steaming process by means of which the sides were flared out, and the addition of high stern and bow pieces, gave them little resemblance to the usual dugout. They were navigable, swift and seaworthy.

It was only in everyday (not ceremonial) dress that the Kwakiutl seem to have been skimpy and plain. Blankets of woven cedar-bark fibers or of furs sewn together seem to have been almost their only clothing in pre-contact times, and until they took over European clothing in the last half of the nineteenth century. Otherwise their products were characterized by abundance or artistry, and for the most part, by both of these qualities.

Social and Ceremonial Life

The Kwakiutl are remarkable for the degree of their preoccupation with social rank and the manner in which every aspect of their culture seems to focus upon this preoccupation. A long series of hereditary social positions was ranked in order of social greatness and intricately elaborated and differentiated by a wealth of titles, crests and ceremonial privileges. Although the positions were hereditary and too few to go around, it was not a static system or one in which participation and interest was limited to the six-hundred-odd position holders. This came about because of the Kwakiutl principle that each position had to be upheld continually by means of property distributions, called "potlatches", and because everyone was involved to some extent in receiving and giving property at potlatches and in the dramatic public and festival nature of potlatching.

For the Kwakiutl the entire winter season was a vacation from economic pursuits and a time of the most intense activity and interest in sociability, potlatching and ceremonial. It was the custom for all the people of several of the Kwakiutl villages to gather by invitation at one village for a long stay. Feasts of many different kinds were held continually. Even during the rest of the year when there were no large gatherings of guests, the Kwakiutl made feasts and social occasions of mealtimes, and during the winter such sociability was increased.

Potlatches of all sorts were held. There were often several in connection with one event such as a winter dance presentation. A man might give a potlatch for his nephew's initiation into the winter dance ceremonial, for the purpose of placing his son in a potlatch office from which he was retiring, or for the purpose of maintaining the standing of his own potlatch position by distributing a greater amount of property than had his rival the year before. In any case the property distribution was an occasion of public moment; the property to be given away was displayed ostentatiously; the potlatch was preceded by announcements summoning the people together; the potlatcher and his speakers made rhetorical capital of detailed histories of potlatching, bragging of past achievements as the property was counted out and the names of the recipients called out. The theme of glorifying the giver of the potlatch at the expense of the recipients and rivals ran through the speeches, the special potlatch songs, and the display of mocking wooden statues. The entire occasion was of maximum interest and excitement for the people.

Lastly, there were the dramatic "winter dances." These had a religious element in that supernatural spirits which had first appeared to certain ancestors, came again to descendants of those ancestors, and old initiates who had had this experience conducted the dances and ceremonials which were the first steps in freeing the new initiates from their state of ecstacy and possession. The religious element certainly heightened the tone of the whole proceeding, but it must be remembered that supernatural spirits appeared only to youths who had the proper hereditary claims to them and, more important still, to those whose sponsors had sufficient property to give the impressive potlatches required at the time of their initiation. The winter dances were probably less religious in character than dramatic. They represent a fully developed theatrical art which provided a heightened occasion for dramatizing social greatness through potlatching. Their theatrical character is apparent in any description of them, or in a mere listing of their prominent features: performances polished by rehearsal, costumed dancers in carved and painted masks of wood, songs and song leaders, an impressive variety of musical instruments, and elaborate stage devices such as trap doors. The performances involved much dramatic tension and much show of violence, for it was a wild and destructive group of supernatural beings that was portrayed.

The vitality and the amount of elaboration which characterized each of these features of Kwakiutl social and ceremonial life can hardly be exaggerated. The hierarchy of individual offices, numayms and tribes; the inheritance of offices and privileges through a number of channels; the highly developed art of carved and painted crests; the process of potlatching; the oratory, art and ritual of the potlatch and the winter dance, were all parts of Kwakiutl culture which were intricately elaborated and detailed and which the people lived out and enjoyed to the full.

Drawing her examples mostly from the winter dance material, Ruth Benedict[1] presented the Kwakiutl as Dionysian seekers after the extreme and violent in experience. Using the accounts of potlatching, she portrays them also as paranoid and megalomanic, a people whose conduct and feelings polarized between triumph and bombast on the one hand, and shame and sensitivity to insult on the other. In this context, Benedict places certain qualities of Kwakiutl personality that have since been given special prominence in the descriptions of Goldman[2] and Ford.[3] Goldman emphasized Kwakiutl competitiveness and Ford emphasized their aggressiveness.

Boas[4] commented briefly on Benedict's picture of the Kwakiutl, both generally as to the difficulty of characterizing a whole people in terms of a leading cultural motif, and more specifically as to the fact that Kwakiutl private life seemed to him to possess many "amiable" features. The Kwakiutl do seem to have many of the qualities Benedict names for them: vigor, zest, violence, jealousy of prerogatives, acquisitiveness, competitiveness, the will to superiority and self-glorification, and great sensitivity to shame. Even in the flagrant case, however, they seem to show more amiable features such as the capacity for sociability and cooperativeness; and traits connected with these are conspicuous features of their private lives as Boas has remarked.

[1] Benedict, 1934.
[2] Mead, 1937.
[3] Ford, 1941.
[4] Boas, 1936 and 1938.

CHAPTER TWO

KWAKIUTL ADJUSTMENT TO THE NEW ECONOMIC CONDITIONS

Economic Adjustment and its Relation to Social Adjustment

The economic life and behavior of the Kwakiutl have been described for us by a series of observers from the 1870's down almost to the present. These observers were interested in the future of the Kwakiutl as members of a culture surrounded by alien conditions. Although the observers themselves were members of the powerful alien culture, and their characterizations were invariably phrased in terms of the ability of the Kwakiutl to be or to become *like* that culture, they add to a general understanding of the Kwakiutl in a way which could not be accomplished by a completely ethnographical focus or by the cumulation of economic-historical details.

Throughout the years, the Kwakiutl are described as industrious but not progressive; as measuring up to almost every standard of enterprise, skillfulness, adaptability and productivity, but as failing to possess these premium qualities in relation to the proper goals, or to be inspired to them by the proper motivations. It is as though the Kwakiutl were able to exploit the new culture to their own ends — a situation almost unique among instances of contact between the so-called civilized and the so-called primitive peoples, and a situation which was clearly exasperating to the Indian agents in particular.

The comments of observers, especially the agents, are often biased and in need of corrective detail, but in spite of distortions, the character of the Kwakiutl emerges sharply out of these judgments of them by outsiders.

The first Kwakiutl agent, Blenkinsop, tells in his 1881 report how the Kwakiutl were in an "apathetic state" out of which "the Agent must endeavour to lift them ere any hope of bettering them can be expected." Their apathy consisted in being "surrounded with boxes of property all ready for the 'potlatch', on which their whole souls are fixed now more than ever."[1] Two years later his report is equally disapproving and somewhat more detailed. In a search for liquor in the baggage of Kwakiutl returning home from the hopfields he had occasion to see the property they had acquired with their earnings and he complains that the proceeds of all their commendable industriousness were certainly going to be used in a way that was not acceptable in the eyes of the surrounding European society:

[1] Canada. Annual Report on Indian Affairs, 1881, p. 170.

> Their property was landed from the steamer "Grace" and subjected to the most searching investigation, but no intoxicants were discovered. They opened their trunks without hesitation, and in these trunks, belonging primarily to the women, were amounts of clothing of the best description, both for themselves and their families.
>
> Eight of these passengers had upwards of $1,500 worth of property. One man alone owned one fifth of this amount, and his purchases included windows, doors and nails . . . a clock and a mirror . . . and a large stock of provisions.
>
> The energy they display in collecting property is certainly remarkable . . . but unfortunately, so much is squandered at feasts and other wise, that they have not as they ought to have, continuous comfort or continuous wholesome food.[2]

In 1885 Dawson remarks: "The difficulties attendant on any effort toward the improvement of the condition and mode of life of the coast tribes of British Columbia are very grave." He thinks that the Kwakiutl along with other groups were at this time "demoralized" by the ease with which it was possible for them to obtain their food from the natural abundance, by the temptations of the towns which offered them the opportunity to get liquor or to make profits on prostitution, and by the lack of "permanent, remunerative work." He concludes: "The problem is fundamentally an industrial one, and is to be attacked, if successfully, from that side. They are naturally industrious enough, and capable, though not so persistently laborious as the whites, and less easy to control than the Chinese."[3] Thus again, it is no lack of industry which hinders their "improvement."

Early in Northwest Coast ethnological work Franz Boas makes similar observations on the general adjustment of the Kwakiutl to the new culture. In the same paragraph in which he comments upon the contribution made by all the Northwest Coast tribes to the economic development of the Province of British Columbia he makes particular mention of the Kwakiutl as a people doomed to certain destruction unless they became more fully accommodated to the new society of the whites surrounding them. In his later writings he never repeats these same observations on the Kwakiutl and it is possible that he revised his opinions once he knew them on their home ground rather than merely as visitors and migratory workers in the town of Victoria. In any case, his first impression of the Kwakiutl was of a people so stubbornly set against the white society that they were likely to fail in spite of their ability to share in the new economic life.[4]

[2] *Ibid.*, 1883, p. 48.

[3] Dawson, 1888, pp. 351—2.

[4] Boas, 1889c, p. 12: Wir sehen hier reichbegabte Völker unter verhältnismäßig günstigen Bedingungen gegen das Andringen der Europäer kämpfen. Ihre ethnographische Eigentümlichkeit wird in sehr kurzer Zeit dem Einfluß der Europäer erlegen sein, und je rascher die Eingeborenen sich in die veränder-

In 1890 the Superintendent of Indian Affairs, E. Dewdney, makes a special point of setting the Kwakiutl apart from the other Northwest Coast peoples in respect to "progressiveness" and prospects for successful future adjustments:

> The Indians of this Province, with but few exceptions, pursued their wonted course of manly independence, intelligent enterprise, and unflagging industry during the past year, . . .
>
> The Kwaw-kewlths . . . have made little or no progress in civilization. It is hoped that the establishment, when effected, in the vicinity of Alert Bay, of an institution for imparting to the young men instruction in some mechanical trades, will serve to stimulate these Indians to make an effort to become useful members of society, and that thus they may be reclaimed in some measure from their present degraded condition.[5]

This judgment on the Kwakiutl in 1890 by a member of the contact culture is consistent with those made in previous years. The lack of "progressiveness" was not a lack of industriousness, but a failure to be industrious for the right reasons, in the context of the values of the whites. Dewdney's opinion along with the earlier opinion of Blenkinsop is remarkable for the false conclusions which the reader is encouraged to draw. These two men could not be reconciled to the fact that the Kwakiutl remained stubbornly and "offensively" themselves in spite of their considerable integration with the industrial and economic aspects of the new culture.

Dewdney implies here that the difficulty is an economic one. This is not supported as one would expect by the details of the 1889–1890 Kwakiutl report in which the Kwakiutl agent notes that the Alert Bay sawmill was giving considerable employment to the Kwakiutl in the vicinity, that an exceptionally good salmon run gave the Indians "full employment," and that logging camps throughout the area afforded further employment. He notes also that the potlatch was operating in full force, that three Indians in the Agency had been arrested for the murder of a white man and two of them sentenced to five years penal servitude, that the behavior of the Indians had been good with one exception caused by the introduction of liquor into a Lekwiltok village, for which the offenders had been fined and, lastly, that the logging camps were "a great snare" in that they offered profits for the prostitution of Kwakiutl women. It is only in this summary of social conditions that Dewdney would be able to find any evidence of "the present degraded condition" and "the lack of progress in civilization" of the

ten Verhältnisse fügen, um so besser sind ihre Aussichten in dem Weltkampfe mit den Weißen. Man kann schon jetzt sagen, daß die Kwakiutl, welche sich vollständig gegen die Europäer abschließen, einem sicheren Untergange geweiht sind. Als Arbeitskräfte haben sich gewisse Indianerstämme bereits unentbehrlich gemacht, und ohne dieselben wurde die wirtschaftliche Entwicklung der Provinz eine schwere Schädigung erfahren.

[5] Canada. Annual Report on Indian Affairs, 1890, pp. xxx—xxxi.

Kwakiutl. In their economic behaviour there is no such evidence, nor is there any situation for which he could realistically propose any economic "cure."

The misleading nature of the reports of these agents was pointed out by the Deputy Superintendent General of Indian Affairs himself, Hayter Reed. In his report for 1895 he states that from what he had observed at first hand the Indians were neither "degraded" nor "backward." Under the heading, *Preconceived Ideas about Indians Corrected by Visiting*, he writes:

> The preconceived ideas about the Indians visited in British Columbia were rapidly dispelled upon coming into contact with them for they were found to be a people more or less independent of eleemosynary assistance from the government, not a few or the most energetic and thrifty possessing a fair share of the good things of this life, and among others particularly comfortable dwelling houses.
>
> In fact many of them appeared to be in better circumstances than a large percentage of white settlers resident in the country. At Bella Bella, Metlakahtla, Alert Bay, Fort Simpson, and Kincolith, houses built after the approved style of the whites, were found, owned by the Indians.[6]

Since Alert Bay is one of the chief Kwakiutl settlements, Reed included the Kwakiutl in his praise and approval. He might well have been impressed with the economic independence of these people in contrast to the poverty-stricken condition of the one-time buffalo hunters of the Plains, for example. Year after year the agency expenditures for Canada indicate that the Kwakiutl as well as other Northwest Coast groups received little if any economic or financial assistance from the government, while in the same years governmental aid was the condition of livelihood for the Indians of many other Canadian agencies. Reed's observation that the Indians seemed better off than "a large percentage" of the white settlers in the area is extremely interesting. Could the visible economic success of the Kwakiutl, in spite of their uncompromising adherence to their own religious and potlatch traditions, have been a source of sufficient irritation to the agents to cause them to label the Kwakiutl as unprogressive and to misrepresent their economic condition?

Ten years later, DeBeck of the Kwakiutl agency makes a report which confirms the picture presented by Reed: apparently the Kwakiutl fit well into the new economic life while remaining aloof from the new way of life as a whole:

> One of the characteristics of these Indians is their opposition to anything and everything advanced by the white man, this is particularly noticeable in their antagonism towards the schools and religious teaching for the children, and can be accounted for to a certain extent by the fact that before the advent of the white man the Indians were great fighting men...

[6] *Ibid.*, 1895, p. xxviii.

> The Indians have been very quiet and peaceable during the past year. I had only one inconsiderable trouble this year, and that was in breaking up their potlatch at Mamamillakulla last April; they seemed to have got the idea that I was interfering with their ceremonies in opposition to the wishes of the department . . .
>
> One might get by casually reading this report the idea that these Indians were a bad lot, or at least that I was trying to create that impression, such, however, is far from being the case. A large majority of these Indians (and I can say it without fear of contradiction) are, in so far as honesty, industry and intelligence go, the equal if not superior of any other Indians on the coast; if they are more immoral or intemperate than others, it is because of their surroundings, their exposure to temptation and the lack of the protection they ought to have. By the latter I mean the inefficient police protection in some portions of the agency and in the cities, towns and municipalities where the Indians are compelled to live during the fishing season, and where it is only on rare occasions we hear of anyone being convicted for supplying the Indians with liquor. There is no place on the North American Continent where Indians can make a living easier than within the bounds of this agency, and there is no doubt in my mind that when they once get into the proper groove they will become good and prosperous citizens.[7]

Halliday became head of the Kwakiutl agency in 1906. His impressions and explanations of the Kwakiutl are like those of Dawson two decades earlier, and he finds the Kwakiutl "indolent and wanting in ambition according to the white man's standard," primarily because "they get their food so easily that 'the spur of necessity' has never been applied to them."[8] Three years later he adds that the Kwakiutl are "averse to being tied down to anything regular" and that they "work hard but not systematically" and that "the idea of the value of a minute has not yet become apparent to them."[9] In both of these reports he notes that the Kwakiutl have been fairly prosperous. In 1909 he makes special mention of the facts that "there is always considerable money in circulation amongst them" and that "they are naturally inclined to any mechanical work." These facts are in contradiction to his picture of the Kwakiutl as lacking in industry, or failing to make any adjustment to the new conditions. In 1910 he summarizes his observations and theories:

> The chief reason for want of progress is the apathy of the Indians themselves. They do not realize that they have sunk into a rut, and only an active effort on their own part can pull them out of it. They make their living very easily, that is so far as the actual necessities are concerned. Fish in one form or another is the chief article of diet, and the waters of the coast teem with fish. Then their ideas of the ideal and that of the whites do not at all correspond. Their chief aim is to go through life easily and get all the fun and glory they can out of it. The glory comes from giving a potlatch, the fun in doing nothing as often as possible. The only hope of improvement is through the education of the young.[10]

Halliday's statement here is clear, and characteristic of many of the preceding evaluations of Kwakiutl adjustment to the new, contact

[7] *Ibid.*, 1905, p. 236.

[8] *Ibid.*, 1906, p. 232.

[9] *Ibid.*, 1909, p. 246.

[10] *Ibid.*, 1910, p. 238.

culture. "Progress" is equated to "becoming like the whites." Kwakiutl are not progressive because "their ideas of the ideal and that of the whites do not at all correspond." Halliday minimized the amount of work and the industrious accumulation of property that necessarily went into the "fun and glory" of a potlatch, but on the basis of his own account it is clear that the Kwakiutl were not, as he claimed them to be, merely indolent and passive recipients of great natural bounty.

The opinions of these contemporary observers contribute to an understanding of how the Kwakiutl reacted to the new economic and cultural surroundings forced upon them by historical developments over this period. Running through the accounts and judgments of the observers is the constant theme that the Kwakiutl were "industrious but not progressive," that their adjustment to the new economic conditions was actually or potentially successful but that it was not impelled by the proper motivations, goals or values.

Since this theme remained a consistent judgment of Kwakiutl behavior from 1881 to 1910, and probably before and after those dates as well, it is likely that it formed an important part of the milieu of outside opinion within which the Kwakiutl lived and worked. It is extremely interesting that the pressures exerted by this climate of judgment are divided against themselves: approval of one aspect of their behavior with reference to the new culture is in conflict with the condemnation of other aspects which was at times both baffled and exasperated. This division of judgment on the part of members of the surrounding culture was one of the factors which made possible the successful adjustment of the Kwakiutl to the new contact conditions, even to the point of exploiting them to their own ends.

Production and Business Methods and Abilities

The Kwakiutl were industrious and able in the production of goods, and acute and skillful in the business manipulation of the goods they produced.[11] Both production and business ability were necessary to sustain the potlatch, which was the financial manipulation of the relations between producers through the institutions of credit and social rank. The potlatch will be discussed later; here the center of interest is the economic activity.

[11] These categories of economic life are similar to the distinctions between subsistence and prestige economy made by DuBois, Herskovits and Bascom. Bascom's additional "commercial economy" applies to the production of a cash crop for the world market with the proceeds of which the natives buy such trade goods as knives. It is not analogous to Kwakiutl "business economy" which is as important a part of the whole native economic life as it later becomes important in relationship with the world market and economy. See Bascom, 1948; DuBois, 1936, pp. 19—65; and Herskovits, 1940.

Production. Measures of productivity – the amount of human energy going into economic production and the ratio of this energy to the economic ends achieved – must be indirect and non-quantitative for the Kwakiutl as for any primitive group. Indeed it is only in very recent years that any kind of statistical measures of economic production and activity are available in our own economy. In the case of the Kwakiutl, there are about one hundred texts collected by Boas, or by George Hunt under the direction of Boas, which are verbatim accounts of the details of Kwakiutl economic processes. They cover all such activities except of salmon fishing, olachen fishing, blanket and mat making, and work in stone. The last of these omissions is unimportant in view of the small part played by stone work in the culture. The omission of salmon fishing from the verbatim accounts is offset by full secondary accounts, and by texts on the curing and storage of fish. The lack of detail on blanket weaving and mat making is perhaps more serious, considering the importance of blankets in the prestige economy of the Kwakiutl. In spite of these omissions, the Kwakiutl texts form one of the richest and most exhaustive sources of economic material in all the literature of anthropology. The very nature of the material assures success in seeing Kwakiutl economic activity in Kwakiutl terms, and analysis of features common to the gamut of economic activities reveals the characteristics of Kwakiutl economic life at its basic producing level.

When all duplications and overlapping are omitted, there are some eighty separate texts available (see Table 2). Two characteristics of Kwakiutl economic life may be discovered from the mere listing of the text titles and topics. First, Kwakiutl economic activities were numerous, various and specialized. These features distinguished Kwakiutl along with other Northwest Coast cultures from other so-called "hunting and gathering" economies; the economic life of the Kwakiutl was complex, rich, sufficient to support a dense population, and concerned with production far in excess of subsistence requirements. Secondly, the Kwakiutl definition of an economic activity was the making of a single product or tool with specialized planned functions, or the procuring of a single natural product, often, as the presence of specific storage techniques and containers indicated, in anticipation of a storable surplus.

TABLE 2[12]

Industries

The making of dishes
Dish for pounding salal berries
The making of boxes
The making of oil boxes
Sewing with cedar withes
Care of canoe

[12] A listing of text subjects relating to Kwakiutl economic activities synthesized from Boas. Unmarked items come from Boas, 1921; *indicates items from Boas, 1909; and ** indicates items in both sources.

Wooden sail
Mat sail and mast
The making of horn spoons**
Cedar bark breaker
Bag of sea-lion hide
Spruce roots and cedar withes
Cedar withes
Spruce roots**
Cedar bark
Cedar mats
Shredding cedar bark
Open-work basket
Cedar-bark basket**
Basket for viburnum berries
Basket for wild carrots
Huckleberry basket
Box for salmon berries
Tump line
Back protector
Belt
Tool for peeling cedar bark
Spade
Digging stick for clover
Digging stick for roots
Digging stick for cryptochiton
Hook for devil fish**
Spear for sea eggs
Elderberry hook
Pole for gathering eel grass
Flounder spear
Fishing tackle for flounders
Fish trap for perch
Net for sea eggs
Stage for drying roots
Frame for drying berries
Rack for holding baskets
Making canoe wedges*
Making a canoe**
Making a paddle*
Making fish hooks*
Making a harpoon*
Making a fish trap*
Preparing cedar withes for baskets*
Preparation of spruce root*
Making a root oven*

Hunting, Fishing and Food Gathering

Goat hunting
Sealing
Catching flounders
Fishing for kelp fish**
Fishing for perch
Gathering herring spawn
Catching devil fish
Gathering seaweed
Digging clover
Digging cinque-foil roots
Digging sea milkwort
Digging bracken root
Digging fern root
Digging erythronium
Digging lupine roots
Digging carrots
Digging lily bulbs
Picking elder berries
Picking salal berries
Picking currants
Picking huckleberries
Picking salmon berries
Picking crabapples
Picking chokecherries
Picking dogwood berries
Picking gooseberries
Halibut and cod fish fishing*
Fishing for red cod*
Hunting porpoise with a harpoon*
Fishing for kelp fish with lines*

Preservation of Food

Cutting dog salmon*
Roasted old salmon*
Middle piece of salmon*
Backbones of salmon*
Fresh roasted backbone*
Pectoral fins of dog salmon*
Dog salmon cheeks
Roasted dog salmon heads
Dog salmon spawn**
Quarter dried salmon
Spawn of silver salmon
Old sockeye salmon
Roasted silver salmon
Salal and elder berries**
Viburnum berries with oil
Split salmon
Sockeye salmon
Halibut
Dried cod
Herring spawn
Currants
Viburnum berries
Crabapples
Qot!xole
Qot!xole with oil
Curing seaweed**
Boiled huckleberries

Of these texts, three-eighths are concerned directly with the collection of food. When such industries as the making of fish hooks, with a direct although secondary relation to food, are included with food preparation and storage, three-fourths of Kwakiutl economic activities are seen to have had food production as their end.

It is in food production that the division of labor between men and women is interconnected and cooperative to the greatest degree. Almost one half of the texts concerned with food production specify that a particular activity was carried out by "her husband" or "his wife," and the work and skills of the two as an economic team were necessary. Most often the man made the tools, digging stick, drying stages and containers necessary for the collecting work of the woman, but in some cases the woman made or collected objects necessary for the man's work, such as fish lines, bait, cedar-bark packstraps, and mats. The texts indicate clearly that men and women were equally occupied and important in the production of food. In manufactures, on the other hand, the work of men and women was sharply divided. Men worked with wood and women with fibers. The major raw material for both wood and fiber was the red cedar, *Thuya gigantea.*

The reproduction of more than a sample of this text material, or its minute cultural-linguistic analysis, is unnecessary for an understanding of its manifest economic content. Two of the shorter translations are given here as examples of the detailed nature of the material on which the later generalizations are based.

> Cedar-Bark (2). — The woman goes into the woods to look for young cedar trees. As soon as she finds them, she picks out one that has no twists in the bark, and whose bark is not thick. She takes her hand-adz and ... cuts the back of the bottom of the young cedar. She leaves a strip four finger-widths wide, which she does not cut when she cuts around the tree, and she peels off a strip two finger-widths wide. This is what the women who get cedar-bark call "making a road", for after that she peels off a broad strip which is to go high up. After she had taken off the narrow strip which makes the road, she begins to peel at the lower end, starting with her adz at the place where she cut around. The broad piece is one span wide. Then she peels it off, and as it goes up high, she steps back from the place where she stands: and if the young cedar-tree is smooth high up, she goes far back.
>
> While she is going backward, she holds slack the cedar-bark that she is peeling off, when it falls back to where it was before. Then the woman who peels the cedar-bark pulls at it, so that it comes off. What she is peeling off becomes narrower as it goes upward, and it just runs into a point and breaks off when it reaches way up. Immediately the woman puts it down on the ground, with the inner side downward, and the outer bark outside. Then she peels off other pieces as she did the first one; and she stops peeling when a strip four-fingers wide is left on the cedar-tree. This is what the people of olden times refer to as being left on the young cedar-tree, so that it should not be without clothes and to keep it alive.
>
> As soon as the woman has enough, she takes up at the broad end what she has peeled off, and she breaks off the outer bark for a distance four spans

in length. She goes on peeling off the outer bark towards the narrow end, and she continues doing this until she reaches the narrow end. When the outer bark has been taken off, she folds it up, and she measures a length of four spans. Then she folds it over. In folding it she places the outer side outside. She first folds the broad end and after she has gone the whole length, she ties the narrow end around it; and she does the same with the others which she has peeled off. As soon as all have been tied in the middle, she takes a long narrow strip of cedar-bark and puts it around each end in this way. After she has done so, she takes another piece of cedar-bark and puts it on as a packing strap. The two packing straps are tied to the two end ropes; and she just measures it until it is long enough when she puts her hands through, carrying it on her back. In her hand she carries the adz, and she goes home to her house.[13]

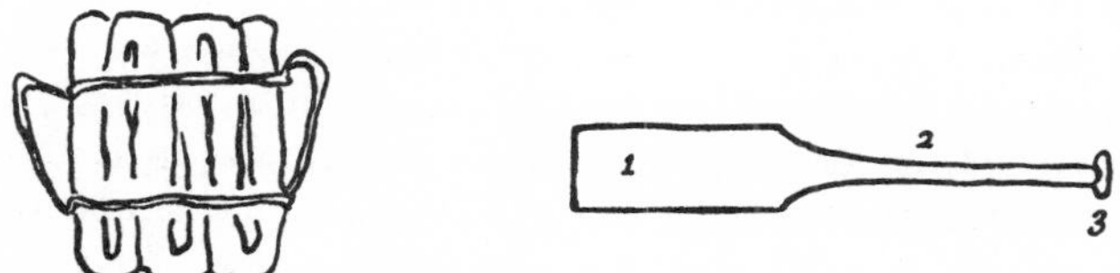

Fig. 2. Manufactures: left, pack of green cedar bark; right, spade for digging lily bulbs (after Boas, 1921).

Spade. — Her husband makes the spade for digging lily-bulbs. It is also chopped out of yew-wood. When he goes into the woods and he finds (yew trees), he chops down one that is two spans in diameter. When the tree falls, he measures off two spans and chops it off with his axe. After he has done so, he splits it through the heart. He takes the side without branches and chops off all the heart-wood so that it comes off and so that it is flat. After he has done this, he chops the other side so that it is two spans thick, and he chops it well until it is smooth and of the same thickness. After doing so, he measures one short span and chops it so that it is this way: and he chops the top so that it has a cross-piece on it. After finishing one edge, he does the same with the other edge. Now the end, beginning at the bottom (1) is square. This is the digging-point, which extends to (2), the middle handle, and towards (3), the cross-piece on top. After doing so, he carries it in his hands as he goes home. He puts it down and takes a piece of fire-wood, on which he adzes it. He takes his adz and takes hold of the spade for lily-bulbs. With his left hand he holds it by the point, and he places the cross-piece (3) on the fire-wood. In his right hand he takes the adz, and he first adzes down at the middle handle (2), which he makes round. When it is round, he turns the end so that the point (1) stands on the fire-wood and he adzes it, so that the point becomes thin like an adz ... As soon as this is done, he takes his crooked-knife and shaves it off so as to make it smooth. Now the digging-point is sharp; and he smooths the cross-piece on top by shaving it. As soon as he has done so, he hardens it by means of tallow. You know the way it is done with the digging-stick for clover when it is heated by the fire and rubbed with tallow to make the point brittle. He does the same way when he is making the spade for lily-bulbs when he is hardening the point of the spade that he is making.[14]

[13] Boas, 1921, pp. 130—132.
[14] *Ibid.*, pp. 144—146.

These two text translations illustrate many of the characteristics of Kwakiutl economic life, and are representative of Kwakiutl procedure in manufacturing. The man was concerned with wood carving, the woman with collecting bark for fiber work. The description of the carving of a spade for digging lily bulbs illustrates an outstanding characteristic of Kwakiutl manufacture, the control of the entire process by the producer. This included travel, usually by canoe, to the place where the raw materials were to be found, the collection of the necessary raw materials, the making of the tools associated with working them, and the making of the finished product. Extreme orderliness and consecutiveness of work procedure are manifest in every account of manufacturing and this to a degree which would seem impossible if the only factor involved was the recital to a recorder of how a certain object was made. This factor might of course produce a picture somewhat neater than reality, but the probability of such orderliness in Kwakiutl manufacturing is increased by the presence of certain other features.

One of these is that in each text are to be found the most minutely fixed details of technique. There was never anything unplanned about any part of Kwakiutl wood or fiber work. For example, a man did not simply give a canoe a rough and a fine adzing. He adzed first the "under chin," then the "water cutter," then one side of the bow and one side of the stern, then the opposite side of the bow and the opposite side of the stern, then the bottom. Then he took his large two-handed long-handled adz and adzed across the grain in grooves, again in a definite fixed sequence of sections of the canoe. Then he took his hand adz and went over the whole canoe again in sections. Then he began all over again; again working the sections in sequence.[15]

Another notable feature of Kwakiutl manufacturing was that the product had precisely pre-planned dimensions and functions. This was so much the case that although Kwakiutl measurements in terms of fingerbreadths, short spans (from the thumb to the tip of the first finger), long spans (the full stretch of the hand), and the like, are not refined from our point of view, the resulting product nevertheless might fairly be called a standard product. The spade for digging lily bulbs was such an article. It was specific in function and of standard measurement within the range, not very great, of variation in the "spans" of the hands of mature Kwakiutl men. Cedar bark, for example, the basis for manufacturing anything from cedar fiber, was carefully collected in strips *one span wide*. All the objects of Kwakiutl manufacture, spoons, blankets, houseboards, canoes, boxes, baskets, fishhooks, fishtraps, pack straps and so forth were, in this somewhat rough and ready sense, standardized products. Although Kwakiutl manufacturing did not make

[15] Boas, 1905a, pp. 359—60, 410—413.

use of machines and jigs and scales in fractions of an inch or meter, it must be emphasized that the orderly and precise procedures resulted in a high degree of standardization in the end products.

It is necessary at this point to consider briefly the characteristics of Kwakiutl production in relation to the natural environment. The Kwakiutl did not merely meet the demands of the geographical environment or make a mere adaptation to the natural surroundings. Instead, the picture is one of a rich environment being exploited to the fullest extent by an energetic population in possession of a whole battery of collection and storage inventions. The Kwakiutl amplified and refined food-getting and storage techniques. In a region where subsistence demands could have been met easily by concentration on getting and storing enough of a few natural products such as salmon and berries, the Kwakiutl chose the grand manner in production as well as in the great displays, distributions and even destructions of wealth so distinctive of their culture. With but few omissions such as snakes, deer, wapiti, many metals and minerals, and some sea and land plants, animals and insects, the Kwakiutl were prepared to acquire in quantity, to utilize, and if appropriate, to store, what was available. Separate techniques and tools were worked out for even rare sea animals such as the octopus, for such sea products as herring spawn, edible seaweed, and kelp, and for the more ordinary range of shellfish, molluscs, sea-eggs and the abundant and dependable varieties of salmon; for the grizzly bear and the mountain goat besides other land animals less difficult and dangerous to hunt, and for a whole array of fruits, roots and berries. Most of the productive energy went into food getting and into the making of the canoes and other equipment associated with food getting. Other types of manufactures, however, placed the Kwakiutl among the best housed and most lavishly supplied, as well as the best fed, of the peoples of the New World. Pluralization was a conspicuous feature of much of this manufacturing. Each household made and possessed many mats, boxes, cedar-bark and fur blankets, wooden dishes, horn spoons, and canoes. It was as though in manufacturing as well as in food production there was no point at which further expenditure of effort in the production of more of the same items was felt to be superfluous. This is entirely consistent with the practice of using many of the food products and manufactured products in the displays and rivalries of the potlatch, and it will be seen later that high level productivity and the potlatch were mutually supportative and stimulating.

Every one of these characteristics of Kwakiutl economic life at the production level is of outstanding importance in attaining a clear understanding of the relation of Kwakiutl to the new contact culture of western Europe and North America. Kwakiutl habits of industriousness, the Kwakiutl assumption that production aimed at a surplus, the Kwakiutl tradition of the "independent operator" – all were potential for success in the new economic setting. The extractive industries of lumbering and fishing were to become the most important industries of coastal British Columbia. For the former, the woodworking skill of Kwakiutl men was as good preparation as was the Kwakiutl emphasis on the production of a food surplus for the latter. The Kwakiutl manufacture of standardized products bears a clear relation to their ideas on the valuation of goods, on their acceptance of blankets and then of money as standards of exchange and payment for labor.

Business methods. The Kwakiutl were economically self-sufficient.[16] They supplied their own goods and, in the potlatch, their own economic drama. It is, therefore, in their relations with the contact culture that evidences of their business astuteness, and their skill in manipulating economic goods according to economic processes and relations, reveals itself. There is no doubt that this astuteness and skillfulness is present to an even more elaborate degree in the potlatch, but there it cannot be clearly seen as such; rather it is allied with a number of complicating and enriching factors. The contact culture forced itself upon them, and their business skills are revealed in their ability to manage the new situation and even in some cases to exploit it.[17]

The first reported contact of Europeans and Kwakiuṭl was at the Lekwiltok village of Cape Mudge, which Vancouver and his party came upon in the circumnavigation of Vancouver Island. This meeting seems to have been conducted with an almost unbelievable courtliness. According to Vancouver: "A few of the Indians accompanied us in our walk, picking the berries from the trees as we passed, and with much civility presenting them to us on green leaves." However, time was

[16] Dawson, 1887, p. 2. He states that "the Kwakiool have no trade routes to the interior, such as those in possession of the Bilhoola and Tsimshian." In the Kwakiutl area the passes into the area were not as easy as those in the areas of the two groups mentioned. However it must be remembered that the Kwakiutl had extensive settlements on the mainland. If Dawson is correct in stating that they did no trading from these settlements and there is such scanty evidence of trading as such in pre-contact times, then it seems safe to argue that trade was relatively unimportant in pre-contact times, that their real center of interest was the potlatch which did have distributing and redistributing functions not however properly called trade; and that trade with Europeans was carried on with some enthusiasm because it could and did support the potlatch system. All of these points will be discussed later in their proper context.

[17] The Kwakiutl share the quality of business astuteness with other of the cultures of the North Pacific Coast. Although only the Kwakiutl material is strictly relevant here it may be noted as corroborating evidence that members of various Northwest Coast cultures were quick and canny in trade and so difficult to exploit that they were exasperating to Europeans and Americans used to economic dictatorship over "simpler" peoples. This may have been partly responsible for the violence which was so frequent in the early maritime fur trade.

found for trade as well as for civilities and gift presentations, and Vancouver was careful to note that several of the natives brought fish and wild fruits "which they exchanged for our European articles in a very fair and honest manner."[18]

The party moved up the channel to the Nimkish village of Alert Bay, and Vancouver gives fuller and more revealing observations on the character of the Kwakiutl in trade relations:

> Cheslakees had no less than eight muskets . . . all kept in excellent order; these, together with a great variety of other European commodities, I presumed, were procured immediately from Nootka, as, on pointing to many of them, they gave us to understand they had come from thence, and in their commercial concerns with us, frequently explained, that their skins would fetch more at Nootka than we chose to offer . . . They were well versed in the principles of trade, and carried it on in a very fair and honorable manner.[19]

Menzies' discussion of this same incident adds further detail to a picture of the Kwakiutl as hardheaded and skillful in business:

> The number of Inhabitants in this Village we estimate about 500 & their commercial intercourse with the Natives of Nootka by some inland communication was pretty evident from their own accounts, for they assured us of having received from thence most of the articles of European Manufacture in their possession, so that it appears extremely probable that this is the Channel by which that post has been of late years supplied with a considerable share of its fine Fur from the Northern regions, for they are well acquainted with traffic and the value of their own commodities, but in their dealing seem to act fair & honest. Upwards of 200 Sea-Otter were procured from them during our short stay at more than double the value I ever saw given for them on any other part of the Coast, consequently many of our Articles of commerce begin now to lose their intrinsic Value amongst them. Iron though valuable to most other Indian Nations was here scarcely sought after. The articles they most esteemed were Sheet Copper & coarse broad blue Cloth.[20]

Both Vancouver's and Menzies' reports picture the Kwakiutl on their first direct contact with Europeans as sophisticated and able in business relations; this to the extent of knowing and exploiting the market conditions of a considerable area in order to get the highest possible prices for their furs and also of having very definite ideas about the adjustment of the prices of various European articles to the supply made available to them and to the number of articles already in their possession.

Material of later date not only confirms this picture of Kwakiutl business ability, but also indicates its scope and the degree of its competence and vigor. The Hudson's Bay Company apparently found the Kwakiutl

[18] Vancouver, 1798, pp. 337—339.
[19] *Ibid.*, p. 348.
[20] Newcombe, 1923, p. 88.

to be real competitors in business, no small tribute to the Kwakiutl. Douglas writes to his Company superiors in 1838:

> The absence of opposition enabled us to suspend the sale of ammunition and firearms in all the Harbours south of Ft. McLoughlin; as a check upon the native Coquilt Pedlars who by the traffic in these articles, with the Indians of Ft. Langley, undersell the Tariff of that Post, and do much injury to its business.[21]

One of the more amusing episodes of economic enterprise in this area involves the first discovery of coal on Vancouver Island at the place later to be called Fort Rupert. The Hudson's Bay Company had been importing Welsh coal for its steamers and shops, and the discovery of local supplies promised decreased costs and possible extra profits in supplying the needs of the American settlements to the south. In 1836 the coal at Beaver Harbor, the site of the later Fort Rupert, was found to be plentiful and of good quality. There were two problems in making use of it.

The first, as Finlayson reports it, was that the company would have the unprofitable expense of building a large fort and maintaining a large defense force to protect the projected mining establishment from the attacks of, not the resident Kwakiutl, but the northern groups who often attacked the Kwakiutl. This fear was groundless, as was proven by the Company's later experience with Fort Rupert as a trading center.

The second difficulty was not at all hypothetical. The Kwakiutl, who had never mined coal or even used it except occasionally as a pigment, very quickly saw the economic possibilities of such an enterprise for the group which controlled it. Finlayson writes:

> They informed us that they would not permit us to work the coals as they were valuable to them, but that they would labour in the mines themselves and sell to us the produce of their exertions . . .

The Kwakiutl were determined to have the profits from the mines for themselves. It is doubtful whether in the entire history of the Hudson's Bay Company's dealings with "simpler people," they met another case of opposition based on precisely their own kind of profit motives. Finlayson concludes his statement:

> . . . but we know from the indolent habits of the Indians, even if the materials for working it were in their hands that in six months they would not furnish a sufficient quantity for the consumption of a day.[22]

This judgment of the Kwakiutl seems to be based rather upon his irritation with them for having the upper hand in a matter of business, than upon observations of them at work.

[21] *The Fort Vancouver Letters (1825—39)*, p. 244. James Douglas to the Deputy Overseer and Committee.

[22] *Ibid.*, p. 334. Finlayson to McLoughlin, September, 1836.

The impasse lasted about ten years. In 1849 the Company brought out a few coal miners from Scotland who worked the coal seams at the newly established post of Fort Rupert. After the discovery of richer coal seams at Nanaimo, out of Kwakiutl territory, the Fort Rupert workings were abandoned. By the end of 1853 the Nanaimo mines operated by the Hudson's Bay Company had shipped 2000 tons, about half of which had been mined with the assistance of the Indians of that place who were perhaps more docile and less competitive in business than the Kwakiutl.[23]

In 1836 the year of the beginning of the coal incident, the Company had another difficulty in its business dealings with the Kwakiutl, in the form of competition from two American trading vessels, the *Peabody* and the *LaGrange*. The former paid three visits to Newettee, and the latter one visit to this large Kwakiutl settlement on the northeast point of Vancouver Island. Finlayson's complaints about this interference with the Company trade apply to their activities in Alaska and Milbank Sound as well as to Newettee but it is clear that the Kwakiutl are included and that the complaint is mainly that the non-Company ships created a situation which the Indians quickly turned to their own business advantage.

> It is not only the number of skins which these vessels collect, that causes serious losses but the extravagant prices paid for them, as they dispose of the remainder of their cargoes under prime cost rather than be at the trouble and expense of carrying it to China where stowage is an object to them, having to take return cargoes to the States. The natives also, who are very keen traders, will keep their skins for months in the expectation of the reappearance of our opponents unless that we become equally liberal and this course we have been obliged to pursue so as to leave as little for them to pick up as possible.[24]

The Hudson's Bay men had a story which they were accustomed to tell as an illustration of the relations of the Kwakiutl with the Company. John Keast Lord visited Fort Rupert in 1849 about fifteen years after its founding. He commented to the officer in charge on the rusty, dusty and useless condition of the little cannons in the turrets of the fort. The officer laughed and said that there was a tradition that the cannon had once been fired to impress the natives; their response however had been to run after the ball, fetch it back to the fort, and offer to trade it in order that it might be fired again.[25]

[23] Sage, 1930, p. 172.

[24] *The Fort Vancouver Letters* (1825—39), p. 330. Finlayson to McLoughlin, September, 1836.

[25] Lord, 1886, p. 164.

Occupations

The Kwakiutl showed extraordinary flexibility in their adjustment of old occupational patterns to new conditions. Much of their success in maintaining their own culture in the midst of the European culture surrounding them must be ascribed to their ability to adjust to market conditions and to exploit new labor and industrial opportunities. Although they ceased much of their native industry to take over the European tools, utensils and clothing, which they paid for with cash earned in working for the Europeans, they continued to house themselves and, more importantly, to feed themselves. Moreover, a large part of their cash earnings came from an extension of their subsistence activities to the point of specialization.

Occupations connected with the production of a food supply sufficient for their own year-round needs and also for feasting, in addition to trading, were engaged in by the Kwakiutl throughout the historical period. The factors which enabled the Kwakiutl to continue direct food production, the major part of subsistence, in spite of their employment in occupations rewarded with a cash income, were: the great natural abundance of such food sources as the salmon, the seasonal character of food gathering, the excellent techniques for procuring this seasonal abundance in quantity, the especially good techniques for storage of food supply arising from the traditional habituation to the accumulation and storage of a surplus and, lastly, continuous possession of the old fishing stations.

Some idea of the ease of Kwakiutl foodgetting can be gained from the standard complaints of the agents and other observers that the Kwakiutl got their living too easily, and that this was above all else responsible for their failure to abandon their old ways in favor of steady hard work, thriftiness, Christianity, and puritanical sex mores. The 1886 Indian Affairs report states that the Kwakiutl

> experience no difficulty in procuring a subsistence, as the sea affords them an inexhaustible supply of food . . . (This) . . . prevents them from adopting those habits of industry, which always tend to steadiness and sobriety of conduct, and to consequent material wealth and comfort.[26]

Dawson, writing about the same time, makes similar observations:

> It is difficult to induce individuals to abandon their old customs and bad habits, and nearly impossible to prevent them from relapsing from time to time, owing to the fact that they still live promiscuously and herd together with the mass of the tribe. Since the arrival of the whites, the Kwakiool, equally with other tribes, have become in a word, "demoralized". They have lost to a great extent, their pride and interest in the things which formerly occupied them, losing at the same time their spirit and self-respect, and replacing it by nothing. It is comparatively easy at all times to obtain a sufficiency of food, and food is at some seasons, as during

[26] Canada. Annual Report on Indian Affairs, 1886, p. lx.

> the salmon run, to be had in the greatest abundance with very little effort. Beyond this, there is nothing more to occupy their time fully and to keep them out of mischief.[27]

And Halliday, the Kwakiutl agent in 1906, writes:

> On the whole the Indians in this agency are inclined to be indolent and wanting in ambition according to the white man's standard. They are all very anxious to be called great chiefs, but do not care to work with their hands to accomplish this. My own opinion of the matter is that they get their food so easily that the "spur of necessity" has never been applied to them.[28]

In the effort to turn the Indians from their customary mode of life, the policy of the Canadian government was at first highly unrealistic. It was based on the idea that great virtues could be assumed to exist in an agricultural life, and that the Indian could best be "civilized" by being turned into a farmer: the same assumption upon which the Indian policy of the United States government was based. William Spragge, for example, commenting in 1872 on Powell's report on the Indians of British Columbia, suggested that in order to give encouragement to the Indians to become farmers, they should be given ample land reserves. Indian success in farming would be assured, he believed, because good prices for farm products would be paid by the whites of the area who were engaged in mining and other occupations. He envisaged a future in which the Indians would be prevailed upon "to take to the plough, and to rely less upon the chase and the results of fishing sports."[29]

The future worked out quite otherwise for the Kwakiutl, and they never to any degree became agriculturists. In 1890 the agent brought a plough into the southern part of the Kwakiutl agency. Agency inventories show "one plough" in 1898, in 1905, in 1907. After that no plough is listed. The Kwakiutl plough had by that time probably rusted away. Moreover, at no time between 1889 and 1932 did the number of acres of land under cultivation in all of Kwakiutl territory, exceed twenty-three! The average number of acres under cultivation during this period was slightly under fourteen, and was planted to potatoes.

Canadian government policy towards the Indians gradually became more realistic and enlightened. In 1876 the Commissioners appointed to settle the question of Indian lands in British Columbia were instructed to follow a liberal policy towards the Indians. They were ... "officially enjoined as little as possible to interfere with any existing tribal arrangements; and ... they were to be careful not to disturb the Indians in the possession of any villages, fishing stations, fur trading posts, settlements, or clearings which they might occupy, and to which they might be specially attached."[30] In 1878 Mr. Sproat, the sole remaining Com-

[27] Dawson, 1881, p. 351.
[28] Canada. Annual Report on Indian Affairs, 1906, p. 232.
[29] *Ibid.*, 1872, p. 5.
[30] *Ibid.*, 1876, pp. xv—xvi.

missioner after the Commission had been cut for reasons of economy, made a report on the importance of the fishing stations to the Indians, which was both accurate and convincing to the authorities. In it he

> strongly advocates the non-interference by Government with any of the fishing rights or habits of the Indians. He says that the Indian Reserve question and the buffalo question are trifles compared with the fishing question to the Indians in British Columbia.

In this same year Powell of the Victoria Superintendency repeats these views and goes even further in his statements concerning the necessity for keeping Indian fishing stations and lands free from white encroachments, and of legislating and enforcing adequate conservation laws for the taking of salmon by the whites.[31]

The assignment of reserves to the Kwakiutl seems to have followed this realistic policy and to have guaranteed to them the possibility of obtaining the salmon and other fish which were so important a part of their subsistence requirements. Boas in 1887 lists fifty-four reserves assigned to the Kwakiutl and of this total thirty-two are described as fishing stations, the remainder being burial sites, village sites, or unspecified as to use.[32] By the year 1900 an additional forty-two reserves were included in the list, without indication of their use.[33] Even if it is assumed that only the original thirty-two of these were for fishing, it is clear that a large part of the total Kwakiutl reserves were fishing stations, the proportion being between one-third to three-fifths of the total number.

The fishing stations described by Boas are for the most part small. Three-eighths of them are eighteen acres or less, with the median at 38.5 acres. The larger ones, like the next to largest reserve at Knight Inlet of 350 acres, are actually the sum of many smaller areas representing the fishing stations claimed by a number of individual Kwakiutl families and lineages. The size of the fishing reserve had nothing to do with its utility; the important thing was to have a station at a good fishing place, such as Knight Inlet. The governmental assignment of reserves assured a continuation of a very old Kwakiutl pattern, the possession of fishing stations which were often quite distant from village sites and which were used most intensively for a brief period during the height of the salmon and olachen runs.

[31] *Ibid.*, 1878, pp. 16, 68—71.

[32] Boas, 1887, pp. 225—232. The maps given in *Geographical Names of the Kwakiutl* by the same author show in many cases how the total modern reserve must be made up of many separate holdings by the various septs of the various numayms. Map 22 shows the oulachen fish traps, garden beds and berry grounds at the head of Knight Inlet. Omitting those sites which are listed as common property, it can be seen that in the pre-reserve period there were over a hundred separately named and separately held sites at this great oulachen fishing spot.

[33] Canada. Annual Report on Indian Affairs, 1900, pp. 105—110.

Once the possession of their old fishing stations was secure, the conservation problem had to be settled if Indian salmon fishing and subsistence were to be assured. Commercial fishing had begun in British Columbia in the 1870's. It was carried on almost exclusively at the mouth of the Fraser River and was confined almost exclusively to the taking of sockeye salmon.[34] Since the salmon runs of the smaller streams important to the Kwakiutl could not compete with the great Fraser River runs in attractiveness to commercial fishing, Kwakiutl fishing was not directly interfered with.[35] Kwakiutl salmon fishing on the smaller streams was legally protected, and the Indian Affairs reports mention but one instance of serious encroachment. In this case the building of a stationary weir on the Nimkish River by two white men was successfully forestalled by an appeal to the laws relating to conservation and the protection of Indian rights.

Although their fishing rights in the smaller rivers were protected, the Kwakiutl might have been adversely affected by the depletion of the entire supply of salmon in the area as a result of the extensive operation of the commercial fisheries offshore at the mouth of the Fraser and at the head of Puget Sound where the salmon tended to congregate in great numbers before making runs up the various streams. The conservation problem was aggravated by the fact that Canadian and United States jurisdiction over these areas was separate, whereas the problem required a joint solution. This difficulty was recognized as early as 1892 when a joint commission was set up to study the protection of the Fraser River and Puget Sound sockeye. No treaty came out of this arrangement until 1937, and even then an additional eight years were allowed before the regulations were to be put fully into effect.[36]

Meantime, regulations were made in British Columbia which in 1887 forbade such practices as dynamiting the waters, in 1889 guaranteed that the Indians could fish for food at all times, and from 1899 on limited the number of commercial fishing boats. In 1889 the number of

[34] *Ibid.*, 1881, pp. 167—8.

[35] The schedule of salmon runs on the Fraser is as follows: (i) Spring salmon *(Oncorhynchus tschwytscha)* June 1 to well on in August; (ii) Sockeye salmon *(Oncorhynchus nerka)* July 1 to the first half of September, the height of season in August, 1—10; (iii) Cohoe *(Oncorhynchus kisutch)* August 1 to the latter part of September; (iv) Pinks *(Oncorhynchus gorbuscha)* last two weeks of August; and (v) Chum *(Oncorhynchus keta)* October 1 to the latter part of November (Howay, Sage, and Angus, 1942, p. 319).

It can be seen that the employment of the Indians by the commercial fisheries and canneries during the time of the sockeye run would not mean that they could do no fishing for themselves. The Spring salmon was at least equal to the sockeye in importance to the Indians. Charles Nowell, sometime after 1905, says that he worked at the canneries at Rivers Inlet "just for the sockeye season" (Ford, 1941, p. 192).

[36] Howay, Sage, and Angus, 1942, p. 378.

boats on the Fraser had been cut from 6000 to 2500 principally by excluding American fishermen, and in 1905 boats on Rivers Inlet were limited to 550 in number.[37]

It is difficult to assess the effectiveness of these regulations. They were not paralleled by regulations on the American side of the international boundary but they were enforced on the Canadian side in spite of what must have been tremendous pressure from an industry whose expansion was important to the whole economy of the Province. Some measure of the rate at which it was growing can be seen in the official valuation of the British Columbia fisheries (Table 3).

TABLE 3[38]

Value of British Columbia Fisheries (1900–1946)

	Value in Millions of Dollars
1900	$ 4.5
1910	9.7
1920	22.3
1930	23.1
1940	21.7
1946	44.5

The size of the pack is another measure of the extent to which commercial interests were exploiting the salmon supply and possibly depleting it so that Indian subsistence would be interfered with. In 1873 two companies on the Fraser packed a total of 8580 cases of sockeye. The number of cases packed in British Columbia in the years following is shown in Table 4.

TABLE 4[39]

Size of British Columbia Salmon Pack (1880–1917)

	Pack in thousands of cases
1880	61
1890	411
1900	606
1910	760
1917	1577

The upshot of the matter seems to be that while the early prodigality of the runs in the salmon streams was reduced there was still sufficient for the Indians. Early stories of the phenomenal abundance of salmon

[37] Short and Doughty, 1914, pp. 445—462.

[38] Compiled from *Canada Year Books* of the Dominion of Canada, Bureau of Statistics.

[39] United States Federal Trade Commission. Report on Canned Foods, Washington, 1919, p. 14.

in Kwakiutl streams are not duplicated in later years. Mayne reported that in the early days of Fort Rupert, founded in 1849, the Hudson's Bay Company used some 3000 salmon yearly as fertilizer for their vegetable garden.[40] Sheldon, writing in the early 1900's, described the run in one of the streams in Kwakiutl territory even at that late date as prodigious: "a creek not over fifty feet wide and very shallow resembled a solid black mass in aggregate motion . . . the trail led along the creek, where the stench of dead and decaying salmon, lying in hundreds on the banks and caught among the driftwood tangles, was almost unendurable." To clinch the tale he describes how a small dog was able to swim out, grab a ten pound salmon by the center fin and drag it bodily back to shore for his dinner.[41] If there are no more stories like these in recent years, neither are there any indications that the salmon streams were so seriously depleted as to make it difficult for the Indians to get their living.

Although fishing was by far the most important of the subsistence occupations of the Kwakiutl, it varied in relative importance from year to year as the salmon runs themselves varied, and it was supplemented by a wide range of other activities. In 1883 Blenkinsop, the agent, notes that the Indians of the Kwakiutl agency "have now almost entirely abandoned the chase as a means of obtaining a livelihood."[42] There is no way of knowing whether this refers to the hunting of mountain goat and bear which were once subsistence activities of minor importance to the Kwakiutl. However, this is the final reference to hunting and indicates that this relatively unimportant subsistence activity ceased at a rather early date.

For 1889 Pidcock specifies that two of the Kwakiutl bands were engaged in sealing, and that some members of nearly all the bands were engaged in oulachen fishing at Knight Inlet. In 1895 there was a poor sockeye run on the Fraser but the agent notes, ". . . sufficient fish was, however, had for the demands of the Indians for their winter consumption, and the supply of berries was exceptionally good." In his 1900 report he notes that "so much oulachen oil was made that its price went down to half its usual figure."[43]

In 1903 the next Kwakiutl agent, DeBeck, mentions the drying of seaweed and the gathering and drying of berries along with the drying of halibut. In his 1905 report he gives further details of the preparation of fish, in terms which suggest a certain specialization in native products other than salmon: "The Nuwitti tribe catch, and dry large quantities of halibut with which they supply other bands," and "The Tswatiano,

[40] Mayne, 1862, p. 183.
[41] Sheldon, 1912, pp. 12, 39.
[42] Canada. Annual Report on Indian Affairs, 1883, p. 49.
[43] *Ibid.*, 1889, p. 256; 1895, p. 168; 1900, p. 275.

Mamalillakulla and Stenawkta bands do the same with regard to the olachen fisheries, and the supply of grease, or Indian butter, for all the other bands is obtained from them."[44] DeBeck may have been ignorant of the fact that members of nearly all the groups had fishing stations at Knight Inlet, or it is possible that specialization in subsistence occupations had increased.

Some time after 1905 it is said in the autobiography of the Kwakiutl Chief, Charles Nowell, that feasts are held in the morning or the evening but not at noon, " . . . because that is the time that they are all busy working or fishing or hunting".[45] This would seem to indicate that subsistence activities were still being carried on, and the agent's report for 1907 confirms this by saying that "the chief factor in keeping them (the Kwakiutl) at Fort Rupert is the abundance and excellence of the supply of clams, which is one of their chief sources of food supply."[46] In 1908 Halliday notes that the Kwakiutl were preparing for their annual oulachen fishing. Because he anticipated hard times (owing chiefly to the government's refusal of handloggers' licenses to the Indians) he says that he ". . . prevailed upon them to make unusual efforts to obtain a full supply of their own native foods."[47] It is likely that he was prevailing upon them to do what they would have done during good or bad times in any case.

The subsistence activities of the Kwakiutl seem to have continued to be an important factor. The 1934 annual report draws attention to the severe effect of the depression upon the Indians of British Columbia because of their dependence upon the commercial fisheries for cash income, but makes particular mention of the fact that the Indians have the special and exclusive privilege of taking salmon for food up-stream in rivers where salmon fishing was otherwise prohibited.[48] The implication is that the depression had not reduced the Kwakiutl to real want because of their economic self-dependence in matters of subsistence.[49] Somewhere between 1935 and 1939, basing the date on other events in the autobiography, Charles Nowell and his wife are reported as roasting clams on the beach at Fort Rupert.[50] It is also possible that the agency reports of 1941, 1943, 1944 and 1946 intend to include subsistence fishing under the category of "fishing." Certainly it is known that in 1945 the Thompson and the Salish as far up the Fraser River as Agassiz,

[44] *Ibid.*, 1905, p. 235.

[45] Ford, 1941, p. 193.

[46] Canada. Annual Report on Indian Affairs, 1907, p. 233.

[47] *Ibid.*, 1908, p. 243.

[48] *Ibid.*, 1934, p. 7.

[49] In this connection it should be mentioned that, although no figures of relief expenditures for the Kwakiutl exist in the agency records after 1924, the aid given up to that time was minimal.

[50] Ford, 1941, p. 241.

British Columbia, were doing considerable fishing for food and it is not unlikely that the Kwakiutl have continued the practice down to the present.[51]

The small amount and the indirectness of much of the data on subsistence is understandable when the nature of the activities is considered. Hunting, fishing, berrying and other collecting would involve individual decisions as to where to travel, how long to stay and how much to collect; and as such, no agent or observer would have been able to keep sufficiently close track of them to estimate their extent.

TABLE 5[52]

Kwakiutl Occupations (1836–1945)

Occupation	Earliest and Most Recent Date Given	Comments
Fishing:		
Commercial	1881—1945	Should undoubtedly be dated from the beginning of the canning industry in 1873. Men, women and children employed. The most important source of cash income. Important throughout the period, although activity depended upon the business cycle.
Subsistence	1872—1934	Before 1872, of course, and probably extending to today.
Lumbering	1888—1941	Hand logging very important (1900 till 1908) when demand fell and licenses to Indians were refused. Some employment at logging camps and saw mills throughout.
Fur-Trapping & Hunting	1836—1907	Peak activity was early in this period and very probably before 1836. As late as 1939, however, agency figures on Kwakiutl income list $1,405 for "hunting".
Sealing	1881—1899	Of minor importance.
Farm Labor and Agriculture	1895—1907	Of insignificant proportions: a little labor for whites in 1895; the raising of "a few chickens and a few sheep" in 1907.
Hop-Picking	1887—1897	Has continued up to today, but relatively unimportant.

[51] Observation of the Columbia University Field Party under the direction of Dr. Marian W. Smith, 1945.

[52] This table is compiled chiefly from data in the Indian Affairs Reports of the Kwakiutl Agency. Finlayson, Douglas, Jacobsen, Boas, Mayne, Sheldon, Ford, Dawson (see bibliography) are also used along with such official sources as the Census of Canada and the report of The Board of Inquiry into the Cost of Living in Canada.

Trading	1836—1907	Unimportant. Aside from the 1905 and 1907 references to internal trade in subsistence products, the only other reference is to whiskey selling in 1882.
Mining	1882	One small group worked in the mines at Nanaimo.
Ethnological Work (Informants, Manufacture and sale of ethnological goods for museums and tourists)	1881—1940	Sale of potlatch paraphernalia in 1923 brought $1,415. There seems to have been a small but continuous income in connection with Kwakiutl ethnological identity.
Miscellaneous:		
Prostitution	1858—1907	At peak in British Columbia gold rush. Later, of importance in connection with logging camps.
Guides	1861—1907	
Washerwomen	1889	In the city of Victoria.
Canoe-Making	1889	For sale to other Kwakiutl. There is indication in one source that canoe and paddle making and sale are also recent.
Road Building	1911	A temporary employment important for a short time.
Motor Boat Building and Operation	1907—1943	For sale to other Kwakiutl. For use as sources of income, principally in fishing.
Box Factory	1911	
Stevedoring	1918	
Building Trades	1941	War industries
Structural Steel Work	1941	War industries
Shipbuilding	1943	War industries
Mail Carrying Contract	1907	Only one person employed in each case.
Teacher at Indian School	1907	Only one person employed in each case.

Tabulations of Kwakiutl occupations during the historical period (Table 5), and of the details of Kwakiutl occupations for the year 1907, for which there happens to be considerable information on each of the Kwakiutl subgroups (Table 6), afford some idea of the variety, range and nature of the occupational picture. In order to complete the picture it is necessary to discuss the seasonal character of the activities, the relative importance of the various occupations, the size and composition of the labor force, the occupational flexibility of the Kwakiutl, and lastly the relative importance of the subsistence and the cash incomes.

One of the characteristics of pre-contact Kwakiutl economic life was that it consisted of a regular series of seasonal occupations during each of which some natural product was gathered and processed. Even warfare and winter dances had their seasons, during the hiatus in economic activities. The Kwakiutl months ("moons") are for the most part named

TABLE 6[53]

Kwakiutl Occupations for Tribal Groupings: Type of Employment and Income (1907)

Kwakiutl Bands (Pop. of Each in Parentheses)

Occupations:	Kwashela (49)	Nakwakto (99)	Nuwitti (71)	Kwakiutl (101)	Koskemo, Kwatsino and Kiaskino (87)	Nimkish (139)	Tsawtaineuck (223)	Mamalillikulla (106)	Tanakteuch (102)	Wewaiaikum and Kwiahkah (72)	Klawitsis and Matilpi (104)	Walitsum (34)	Wewaikai (118)	Type of Employment: Source and Nature of Income
Cannery Fishing and Work	$	$	$	$	$	$	$	$	$	$	$	$	$	Non-Indian employers. All cash income amt. of earnings dependent on world economic conditions
Dog Salmon Fishing and Manufacture of Oil	$													
Fishing for Fresh Fish Mkt										$				
Salmon (Trolling for Salteries)......					$									
Olachen Fishing and Oil making ...							$	$	$		$			Self-employed: larger part of produce sold for cash to other Indians, must also add directly to own food supply.
Halibut Fishing and Drying	$	$	$?											
Clam Drying and Smoking			$											
Collect and Cure Herring Roe......								$						
Fishing for own use (winter)	F	F					F		F					Self-employed: income in food for winter use.
Halibut Fishing and Drying	F		F ?											
Logging for Companies				$		$								Non-Indian employers: cash income
Work in Saw Mills						$								
Hand Logging (Self Empld)				$		$	$	$	$	$	$	$	$	Self-employed: cash income amt. depending on world conditions.
Furs (Hunting and Trapping)	$	$			$		$	$	$					
Guides and Packers				$		$								Non-Indian emplys: cash income.
Making and Selling Canoes........			$								$?			Self-emplyd: cash income
Making and Selling Curios.........						$								,,
Prostitution in Logging Camps.....										$				,,
Mail Carrying Contract	$													,,
Poultry: "a few" in both cases					$? F					$F ?				Self-emplyd: income probably in food for own use.

[53] Canada. Annual Report on Indian Affairs, 1907.

after the natural product available at the time, or for the occupation itself, e. g., Olachen-fishing Season, Raspberry Season, Huckleberry Season, Sockeye Moon.[54] In their coastal country with its inlets, islands and fjords, Kwakiutl canoe-using guaranteed an incomparable mobility, and the Kwakiutl practice was to exploit the natural crop at the location and during the season of its greatest abundance.

The seasonal character of Kwakiutl occupations has for the most part continued in the historical period. Of the nineteen occupations given for the various Kwakiutl bands for the year 1907, thirteen are found to be definitely seasonal, two probably seasonal (prostitution in logging camps and guiding for hunters and others), only two are definitely nonseasonal (mail-carrying and poultry keeping), and the remaining two are of the type that could be seasonal by default (making and selling canoes and curios) since they could fit into slack times. A more complete list of Kwakiutl occupations in the historical period adds to the list of seasonal activities, sealing and picking hops in the commercial hop fields. Only the war industries jobs of both World Wars seem to have involved a significantly large proportion of Kwakiutl employees in work of a steady and non-seasonal type.

The seasonal nature of much of the activity of the Kwakiutl explains the fact that many individuals did numerous jobs in the course of a year.[55] It explains also how women and children could be counted as part of the labor force, since many of the jobs were of short duration. There are no actual figures on the number of women and children who worked at the various seasonal employments but in the case of fishing the Agency records leave no room for doubt as to whether they did work. In 1898 the school report states:

> Owing to a poor fishing season the old pupils returned to school at once, and before the end of the quarter, the school was full with twenty-six pupils in attendance. In spite of the repeated requests of the old people for their boys to attend the winter dances, they stuck to their studies very well.[56]

From this it is even possible to conclude that the business of fishing was an even more serious interference with school than the winter ceremonial season.

In 1903 the report specifically mentions the employment of children as well as women in the canneries, while the men did the fishing. Women were also reported as employed in making nets. An indication of the

[54] Boas, 1905, p. 413.

[55] This would explain also the fact that when the number of employees in different categories are added together, the total amounts to about 75 per cent of the population, a highly improbable figure. Full employment in the United States is considered to exist when the gainfully employed are 40 per cent of the population.

[56] Canada. Annual Report on Indian Affairs, 1898, p. 339.

proportion of women to men employees in the commercial fisheries is given by the 1931 Census of Canada; twelve women and 2,926 men were numbered as fishermen, 458 women and 568 men as fish canners and curers.[57]

In the historical as in the pre-contact period, fishing was the most important of the Kwakiutl occupations. It was the source of the main subsistence as well as the main cash income. Employment in commercial fishing, and the cash income received for such fishing, varied with circumstances. In general it followed the business cycles of the United States and Canadian economies. There were many minor fluctuations in the period of industrial expansion from the 1870's to the first World War and the boom which followed it; in 1920–21 there was a sharp recession, in the early 1930's a severe depression, and then a boom in the 1940's.

Another factor in employment and wages in the fishing industry was the periodicity of the sockeye salmon runs on the Fraser River. Of all the salmon streams in the area the Fraser is unique in having a bumper sockeye run once every four years, counting from 1913.[58] If there was increased employment during these bumper years, the price paid per fish was less, and hourly rates for cannery jobs and salaries for Indian foremen of fishing crews tended to remain at a level through the good and bad years, except for the slow upward trend corresponding to the general rise of prices.

A development of special interest in Kwakiutl fishing was the commercialization among themselves of their own fishing surpluses of specialties such as oulachen oil and dried halibut. These may also have been produced and traded in pre-contact times, but in historical times they became the basis for cash sales with possibly greater earnings.

Although figures on the size of the Kwakiutl labor force are available only for 1906–14 (Tables 7 and 8), the statistical evidence on the numerical importance of the fishing industry is corroborated by the verbal statements of the Indian agents. There is no explanation in the agency reports for the extraordinary drop in employment in both "hunting and fishing" and "other industries" in the years 1910 and 1913. Inspection of the table reveals other difficulties; it is wholly improbable that the number engaged in hunting remained exactly the same for the three years beginning with 1907, and the 1911, 1912 and 1913 figures are suspiciously identical for the two categories. It is also probable that individual Kwakiutl are being counted twice, once as

[57] *Ibid.*, 1903, p. 292. Census of Canada, 1931, Vol. VI, Population.

[58] McIntyre, 1914, p. 463.

TABLE 7[59]

Kwakiutl: Number Employed and Earnings (1906—1914)

Date	Pop.	Engaged in Fishing & Hunting No.	Engaged in Fishing & Hunting % Pop.	Earnings from Fishing	Earnings from Hunting	Engaged in other industries	Earnings from other industries	Wages Earned	Total Income
1906	1257	719	56	$37,055	$6,795	103	$12,025	$24,650	$80,985
1907	1305	730	56	56,950	6,300	241	25,100	4,216	93,270
1908	1294	730	56	52,450	4,850	240	40,150	6,160	104,175
1909	1263	730	58	46,300	4,900	235	16,300	6,000	73,500
1910	1238	262	21	44,200	5,800	88	15,700	7,980	73,680
1911	1208	696	54	54,450	5,450	233	20,050	8,300	88,250
1912	1199	696	58	60,700	7,050	233	18,800	12,200	98,750
1913	1186	693	58	95,000	3,870	233	19,350	20,040	138,260
1914	1183	386	34	101,000	2,400	91	10,150	21,525	135,195

TABLE 8[60]

Kwakiutl: Employment and Population By Age and Sex (1906—1914)

		Population										Employment	
		Under 6		6—15		16—20		21—65		65—			
Date	Total	M	F	M	F	M	F	M	F	M	F	Fishing & Hunting	Other
1906	1257	79	73	73	62	51	15	466	378	25	35	719	103
1907	1305	72	69	110	77	42	23	455	400	21	36	730	241
1908	1294	71	64	114	80	43	21	448	398	23	32	730	240
1910	1238	90	103	107	69	29	25	422	344	25	34	262	88
1911	1208	99	87	115	73	29	20	400	338	20	27	696	233
1912	1199	98	90	115	70	33	16	382	338	25	32	696	233
1913	1186	97	90	111	68	33	19	384	338	22	24	693	233
1914	1183	80	73	108	90	31	15	384	340	26	36	386	91

engaged in "fishing and hunting," and once as engaged in "other industries." Certainly the same individuals were engaged in several different types of occupations during the same year. Here as throughout this enquiry such statistics as these are included. When they are in accord with the sense of all the other data, it would be an obvious error in methodology to exclude them on grounds of incompleteness or imperfection. A crude measure is more effective than a vague one from an operational point of view.

The seasonal employment situation with the possibility of the same individual working at a series of jobs in the course of the year, and the existence of a potentially very large labor force because of the inclusion

[59] This table is a compilation of Kwakiutl agency figures as given in the Annual Report of Indian Affairs for Canada for these years. The only addition to the table is the percentage of the population engaged in hunting and fishing.

[60] Compiled on the basis of the reports of the Kwakiutl Agency for these years.

of women and children at times, made for great flexibility on the part of the Kwakiutl in adjusting to any unusual demands for labor or in taking advantage of new employment opportunities.

As early as 1882 the Kwakiutl are said to have answered the great demand for labor in the Fraser canneries and fisheries and to have received high wages for doing so. The following year the same agent, Blenkinsop, claims that the good wages of the preceding year in the canneries and the hop fields would continue to draw them south, especially since the price for furs remained unattractively low in spite of their decreased production. Blenkinsop not only reports them as taking canny advantage of their economic opportunities, but expects this of them and is impressed with the earnings which result. His inspection of what they purchased and brought back with them from their work in the south elicits his admiration: "The energy they display in collecting property is certainly remarkable."[61]

The 1890 report of the Kwakiutl agent notes it as exceptional that the Kwakiutl were too busy with potlatching to go to work in the canneries in spite of "an unprecedented run" of salmon and a great demand for labor in the fall of 1889.[62] In 1891 Pidcock notes that the salmon catch at Alert Bay was "almost a total failure: therefore numbers of them have gone to the hop fields,"[63] suggesting that they were taking advantage of what employment opportunities there were.

Old fields of labor were also extended to meet new demands. In 1889 for example, one group, the Lekwiltok, are reported as making dogfish oil which they then sold at a good price to the logging camps as grease for the logging skids.[64] In 1907 another group of Kwakiutl are reported to have acted upon the suggestion of a white cannery manager, that they should fish for dog salmon for export to Japan.[65] Once again it was a question of their willingness to adjust old skills to new demands.

A less successful attempt of the Kwakiutl to develop a new industry on the basis of their former skills can be found in the logging enterprise which began about 1892 among the Lekwiltok. The enterprise seems to have been boldly conceived to meet the great demand for saw logs arising from the construction of the transcontinental railroad and later from the prairie provinces which the railroad opened and served. The figures on lumber production in British Columbia for successive decades gives the economic background of Kwakiutl operations during these years (Table 9).

[61] Canada. Annual Report on Indian Affairs, 1882, p. 65; 1883, p. 48.
[62] *Ibid.*, 1890, p. xxx and p. 25.
[63] *Ibid.*, 1891, p. 119.
[64] *Ibid.*, 1889, p. 103.
[65] *Ibid.*, 1907, p. 229.

TABLE 9

Lumber Production in British Columbia (1871—1910)

	Millions f. b. m.
1871—1880	350
1881—1890	550
1891—1900	1,327
1901—1910	4,754

The 1901–1910 period shows the greatest production and the greatest increase over previous periods.[66] It was during these years Kwakiutl hand logging was carried on profitably in spite of the handicaps an independent Kwakiutl hand-logger faced in competition with logging companies whose activities, although controlled, were favored in provincial legislation on timber lands.

The difficulties faced by the Indians in their logging operations were largely man-made, and of the sort which they were least able to meet. When the Lekwiltok began in 1892 they cleared between two and three miles of logging roads. The necessity for hiring white men with teams of oxen to haul out the logs that were cut got them heavily into debt and so the agent forbade them to continue operations. If they had been allowed to continue they might have been able to find other means of getting the logs out and to turn into a profit their heavy initial investment, as they did in 1913 when they repaid a government loan granted to make possible the logging of forty acres of their reserve.[67] In view of this situation the comment of the agent in 1891 seems somewhat unjustified:

> . . . the mission saw-mill still affords plenty of work for those who want it, but the young men do not sufficiently appreciate this endeavour for their welfare; they might earn large wages by getting logs, but only a few avail themselves of the opportunity.[68]

That the difficulties of the Indians continued is indicated by the comment of the Kwakiutl agent in 1903:

> In the last year the Indians are paying more attention to hand-logging; in this field of industry there would be a good chance for them were it not that the most of the government timber-lands in this district are either held under lease by the different saw-mill companies or are reserved by the provincial government for pulp purposes.[69]

Two years later the same agent mentions that "quite a number" of the Kwakiutl had gone in for hand logging in spite of the handicaps of being so far from the principal log market, Vancouver, and being "practically at the mercy of one saw mill, the only one in this section of the country or within two-hundred miles."[70]

[66] Howay, Sage, and Angus, 1942, p. 302.

[67] Canada. Annual Report on Indian Affairs, 1892, p. 236; 1893, p. 124.

[68] *Ibid.*, 1891, p. 119.

[69] *Ibid.*, 1903, p. 292.

[70] *Ibid.*, 1905, p. 235.

In the 1907 report, of twelve Kwakiutl groups only three were not mentioned as engaging in hand logging during the previous years. It was declared to be the primary occupation for the "Kwakewlth" and the "Klawatsis and Matilpi" grouped as one; and mentioned as significant among the occupations of each of the remaining groups. The report adds:

> The past year . . . has been a banner year so far as the earnings of the Indians in concerned. The unprecedented demand for logs and the great advance in price has in many instances doubled the earnings of the Indians.[71]

There are no earnings figures available specifically for logging in Table 7, given above, which includes logging in "Other Industries." Between 1906 and 1907 the earnings from "Other Industries" doubled, and between 1907 and 1908 they increased by 60 per cent. Earnings from fishing, a seasonal occupation which does not compete with logging, increased substantially between 1906 and 1907. Aside from this the only significant change in the figures was the decrease in the "Wages" category. Therefore although the earnings figures do not show just how much the Kwakiutl earned from their hand logging, there is every evidence that they chose to engage in this independent, self-employed occupation and that their choice as shown by their total income was profitable.

These favorable conditions held until 1908 when economic circumstances changed, and legislation was passed which would have prevented the Kwakiutl from further profitable activity in hand logging in any case. The provincial government refused to issue any more hand loggers licenses to Indians, and withdrew all timber lands from the market.[72]

This hand-logging episode in Kwakiutl economic history furnishes further evidence of their flexibility in taking advantage of a profitable opportunity. Another example is the ease with which they accepted power driven boats and learned to build and run them. As early as 1907 a member of the Tanakteuch band is reported as owning and running a small steamboat which was used in connection with hand logging; and a Nimkish man bought a two-horse power motor for which he was building a boat. The 1911 report states that the Klawatsis and Matilpi "own several good gasolene boats which they manage well. Throughout the whole agency the motor boat is rapidly superceding the canoe or sail-boat." The 1913 report adds that "Since the introduction of the

[71] *Ibid.*, 1907, p. 240.

[72] *Ibid.*, 1908, p. 243. In this discriminatory legislation Howay, Sage and Angus (1942, p. 309) see "the self assertion of the pioneer." Certainly some similar cause for its enactment must be found, for it is most unlikely that the activities of a small group like the Kwakiutl, for example, were competing seriously with the big companies. The only possibility, and there seems to be no evidence on this point, was that the big companies might find it more difficult to get wage labor if a profitable area of self-employment existed.

motor boat amongst the Indians some of them have taken to building boats, in which they succeed very well." The 1918 report mentions that in that year when earnings were good the bulk of money earned "was put to good purpose" in buying or manufacturing launches and in improving homes. By 1914 it is reported: "Several Indians in the Kwakkewlth Agency purchased seine boats and equipment valued at from $10,000 to $15,000 each."[73]

These statements by agents are confirmed by the figures given in the reports, although, as is often the case, they are difficult to use. Until 1917 the reports list three categories of boats: sailboats, rowboats and canoes. From 1898 to 1914 the number of canoes is far greater than that of the other two categories put together. The number of sailboats probably includes some gas boats from at least 1911 on when the text of the report mentions "several" as quoted above, because from 1917 to 1932 the reports list "motor and sail boats" in the same category.

Except for these agency reports which list the number of sailboats, evidence on their use by the Kwakiutl is negative. The literature does not contain references to them. When Captain Jacobsen made his collection of Northwest Coast ethnographical objects for the *Museum für Völkerkunde* in 1881–1883 one of his qualifications for the job as his German backers saw it was that he was a formidable sailor and could therefore travel freely and independently in the intricate coastal waterways of this area.[74] He rented his sailboat from the Hudson's Bay trader at Fort Rupert not from an Indian when he travelled in Kwakiutl territory, and his way of travelling earned for him the Kwakiutl potlatch name "Einer, der von einem Stern zum andern läuft," (One who travels from one star to another), a name which fits a sailor-navigator of a sailboat at the same time as it singles one out as somewhat remarkable among the Kwakiutl.

The category of motor and sailboats numbers 126 in 1917 and increases to 155 for the years 1928 to 1932. The other category which includes canoes and rowboats decreases from 362 in 1917 to 237 in 1931. The per capita number of boats of all kinds remains about the same throughout the entire period from 1897 to 1931, approximately 2.5 people per boat. It is the increase in the number of motor and sailboats (in which category the apparent unimportance of sailboats must be taken into consideration) against the decrease in the number of canoes which gives a definite indication of the increasing importance of motor boats.

[73] Canada. Annual Report on Indian Affairs; 1907, pp. 234, 238; 1911, p. 228; 1913, p. 224; 1918, p. 38; 1944, p. 149. The 1918 figure applies to all the Indians including the Kwakiutl in southwestern British Columbia. The Kwakiutl must have constituted an important section of this group.

[74] Jacobsen, 1884, pp. 46, 127.

There is evidence that the Kwakiutl made a speedy and flexible adjustment to the motor boat. They learned to build hulls suitable for gas engines and to maintain and run the motors. They saved up for, and made considerable investment in, motor boats. They used them alike in the old traditional patterns in which they to a certain extent replaced large canoes as a means of transporting large numbers of people, and in the new enterprise of seine fishing. They were quick to realize new economic opportunities in so far as they could enhance old economic patterns of efficient, seasonal, self-employed and profitable activity.

The increasing importance of the gasoline launch among the Kwakiutl is indicated in its use on ceremonial occassions as well as economic ones. Whether it actually replaced the large sea-going canoe in the formal pageantry of travels to another village for potlatches and other ceremonies is difficult to know, but in 1921 on the occasion of the death of his brother, Charles Nowell sends out three gas boats "to call the people together, telling them that the chief is dead, and that we Fort Ruperts and Nimkish are not able to bury him by ourselves." He says that the tribes all came the same day, suggesting that they must have used gas boats to come so quickly. This seems all the more likely in that the year before when Charles Nowell's son Alfred died, the tribes came to his funeral "in their gas-boats – three or four gas-boats coming tied together – the people . . . singing their songs".[75] In this instance the gas boats were lined up and tied together on approaching their destination in exactly the same manner as had been customary in making a formal arrival at a village by canoe.

The success of the Kwakiutl in adjusting to the new economic conditions can be set in clearer relief by considering the size and character of the labor force with which they competed. The total population of British Columbia in 1931 was somewhat less than 700,000. Included in this figure were more than 45,000 Chinese and slightly more than 22,000 Japanese. The Kwakiutl at this time numbered slightly over 1,000.

In commercial fishing, one of the most lucrative of the occupations in which the Kwakiutl engaged, they competed with White and Japanese fishermen and with Chinese cannery workers. Chinese are mentioned in 1888[76] and the Japanese also began to figure as important in the labor force. In 1895 the Indian agent said, "In former times nearly the entire work at the canneries was, with the exception of a few Chinese employees, monopolized by the Indians; but the advent of the Japanese and others in later years, has to some extent lessened the earnings of those Indians engaged in the prosecution of that industry."[77]

[75] Ford, 1941, pp. 216, 219.
[76] Dawson, 1888, p. 352.
[77] Canada. Annual Report on Indian Affairs, 1895, p. 168.

In spite of the continuous presence of Chinese, Japanese and Whites in the fishing industry, the Indians continued to be important. In 1924 Duncan Scott writes in the *Handbook of Canada* that in British Columbia the Indian "is a highly important factor in the labor of the salmon fishery, not only in the taking of the fish, but in the preparation in the canneries of the produce for the market."[78] In 1934 the Indians, including the Kwakiutl, were still apparently meeting successfully the competition of other groups. The annual report for that year commenced:

> In my previous annual report I drew attention to the particularly severe effect of the depression on the fishing Indians on the West coast of British Columbia. They comprise a population of upwards of 10,000 aborigines. The men catch the fish for the canning companies, while the women find employment in the canneries. The Indian fishermen hold their own well with White and Japanese competitors.[79]

In 1936 the Kwakiutl met difficulties with their white competitors in commercial fishing. Rivers Inlet was a center for Kwakiutl fishing at this time, and over a hundred Indian boats were affected by a strike of White fishermen in this area. The Indians did not wish to participate in the strike, and asked permission of the canneries to fish. The canneries however refused to issue nets to the Indians out of fear that the nets, valued at $130 each, might be destroyed by the White strikers. The Indians were therefore unable to earn anything, even enough to finance their return home from the fishing grounds.[80]

In 1941 the agency report speaks of "severe competition from foreigners" in the fishing industry. Again in 1946 it was said of all the Indians in British Columbia that "the prosperity of the war years and absence of Japanese competition continued with great benefit to those Indians engaged in the fishing industry." Salmon fishing ended late in October in the Kwakiutl agency and all Indian fishermen concluded the season with a fair catch and return for their labor. Herring fishing was also good.[81]

It seems clear that although the Kwakiutl since before 1900 met real competition from other groups in the labor force engaged in commercial fishing, and although there were times when their earning possibilities were interfered with or lessened, on the whole they were able to meet this competition and they were to no great extent pushed out of the fishing industry. Certainly one of the most severe tests of their success in meeting new occupational demands or in adjusting old occupational patterns to new conditions was their competition for jobs in commercial fishing, with the White, Chinese and Japanese groups which far out-

[78] British Association for the Advancement of Science, *Handbook of Canada*, 1924, p. 17.

[79] Canada. Annual Report on Indian Affairs, 1934, p. 7.

[80] *Ibid.*, 1936, p. 102.

[81] *Ibid.*, 1941, p. 162; 1946, p. 197.

numbered them. It was a test both of their skill in fishing and of their whole economic and occupational organization and it was successfully passed. This will be still more clearly seen in the income material which follows.

Income

The increase in the money income of the Kwakiutl during the first two decades of the twentieth century was a major factor in the historical development of Kwakiutl culture. Per capita earnings increased from $54 in 1903 to $244 in 1921, more than quadrupling in twenty years. Except for two years during the First World War, the series of income figures is unbroken. Following a recession in 1921–22 the income again increased slightly although never again reaching the earlier peak. There was another low point in 1934 when income fell to $34 per capita, but by 1939 it had risen again until it was nearly at the boom levels of the 1920's.

First of all it is necessary to assess the significance and to explore the meaning of the per capita figures available for the Kwakiutl. Figures on national income and per capita income have not been available annually even for the United States until very recent years, being compiled for the first time in the 1930's. That such figures exist for the Kwakiutl agency from the beginning of the century is a fortunate circumstance and probably an accidental one, depending on such factors as the careful account keeping of the Hudson's Bay personnel whose relations to the Indians antedated those of government officials, at the same time as they laid down a pattern of procedures.[82]

The next question relates to the reliability of these figures on income. Attention has already been drawn to certain difficulties in interpreting agency figures.[83] The figures for total income, and the per capita income computed from the total, are probably more reliable than the figures for the separate categories of income. Table 10, in which the income is shown by categories, seems to indicate that incomes from fishing and wages are often confused, for example. The 1906 and 1907 figures show clearly that the marked drop in wages is adequately compensated for by an increase in income from fishing. Perhaps this mixing of categories occurred when a new agent, Halliday, came into office in 1906.

[82] In British Columbia particularly there was a great deal of continuity between the Hudson's Bay policies and those of the later government of British Columbia as a Crown colony. James Douglas for example was appointed governor of British Columbia in 1858. He, an important Hudson's Bay Company official, had much to do with the formulation of a policy towards the Indians of British Columbia, quite different from that of the rest of Canada or the United States. The first Agent of the Kwakiutl Agency, George Blenkinsop, was a former Hudson's Bay man. See Macleod, 1928a, pp. 480—83; Howay, Sage and Angus, 1942.

[83] See pp. 35—6.

The most difficult question is whether a significant proportion of the money income reported as from fishing and hunting, especially from fishing, consists of a money valuation which the agent has placed upon Kwakiutl subsistence products. There is no statement in the official Canadian reports as to how such figures were compiled. Indeed it is clear from the forms that they fit an agricultural group far better than a fishing group such as the Kwakiutl. It is for this reason, for instance, that we have inventories of agricultural tools which are so insignificant in number in the Kwakiutl agency that to list them is ludicrous. Until the year 1914 the categories of both fishing and hunting are headed "Fishing for food" or "Fishing and hunting as food." After 1917 the categories are headed "Earned by fishing" or "Earned by trapping." The *Canada Yearbook* notes in 1918 that figures for Indian earnings from fishing and hunting include an estimate of the value taken for the Indian's own food. In 1921 there is no notation to this effect. In spite of these notations the amount of the income totals coming from an estimate of subsistence products are probably insignificant. The totals given for any year in any category of income are made up primarily of cash income. (Table 10.)

It has been shown that the Kwakiutl continued important subsistence activities throughout this period and that this part of their economic life was carried on by intensive activities in various fishing sites, berry patches and the like, which were widely scattered throughout their territory. The difficulty of getting data on the amounts of such produce as they collected, to say nothing of the difficulty of assigning a money value to them, would be great. For the most part the Kwakiutl agents seem to have made only one yearly trip to each of the Kwakiutl villages and settlements. It does not seem likely that they would have been able to collect information under these conditions. Furthermore, there is no sign in their reports that they have assigned an arbitrary money value to the subsistence income. Such arbitrary valuations ordinarily show up in a population or income series as a base which remains improbably the same over a period of years.

The internal evidence suggests that the agents were dealing with money income which tended to fluctuate very widely from year to year, as it also tended to follow the main trends of the United States and Canadian business cycles. In any case, the wide yearly fluctuations could certainly not be accounted for by variations in the subsistence income. The figures in the Kwakiutl earnings table seem therefore to be primarily of cash income, and the per capita income figures must also be thought of as per capita money income. This is of the greatest importance in understanding Kwakiutl behavior in relation to the potlatch, and the changes in Kwakiutl culture arising out of a greater emphasis on potlatching.

TABLE 10[84]

Kwakiutl Income (1903—1939)

	Wages	Fishing	Hunt-ing	Other indus-tries	Rents			Annui-ties	Total
					Timber	Not specfd.	Land		
1903	$31 005	$26 450	$7 150	$8 200					$73 033
1904	30 860	29 190	6 200	7 200					73 990
1905	26 450	34 125	6 575	7 800					75 397
1906	24 650	37 055	6 795	10 025					80 985
1907	4 210	56 950	6 300	25 100					93 270
1908	6 160	52 450	4 850	40 150					104 175
1909	6 000	46 300	4 900	16 300					73 500
1910	7 980	44 200	5 800	15 700					73 680
1911	8 300	54 450	5 450	20 050					88 250
1912	12 200	60 700	7 050	18 800					98 750
1913	20 040	95 000	3 870	19 350					138 260
1914	21 525	101 000	2 400	10 150					135 195
1917	14 150	97 500	1 800	17 200					131 789
1918	15 200	94 500	1 900	22 200		$ 120			133 954
1919	20 150	144 500	1 450	27 050		495			194 812
1920	27 950	182 500	7 850	31 500		5 120			256 138
1921	26 200	201 700	3 500	43 700		120			276 590
1922	18 750	48 000	6 430	48 900		1 662		$1 526	125 678
1923	22 650	60 200	5 700	50 600	$14 736		$1 324	1 347	156 809
1924	30 900	62 700	5 850	60 900	2 167		390	1 291	164 468
1925	27 900	123 400	5 650	27 500			620	1 388	188 748
1927	28 500	110 600	5 800	11 900	1 252			1 352	160 045
1928	15 350	60 000	3 900	6 950	10 373		440	1 268	98 882
1929	11 300	55 300	3 600	1 577	3 253		760	1 577	78 940
1931	11 950	53 900	2 400		2 662		740	1 472	73 124
1932	3 450	48 300	2 100	300	1 735		560	1 535	58 480
1934	3 700	23 230	2 780	3 580	160		440	2 168	36 858
1935	4 100	28 100	1 410	6 000	12 718		240	3 012	55 586
1936	8 600	113 790	3 085	8 900	9 215		530	3 428	
1938	7 300	101 500	1 035	32 800	14 089		917	3 819	162 022
1939	9 370	88 850	1 405	26 000	12 462		925	4 167	145 525

[84] *Ibid.*, 1903—1939. The totals as given by the Indian agents do not always equal the sum of the different categories of income.

When the figures for Kwakiutl income are considered by categories, fishing is seen to be the most important source of income, as would be expected from the material on occupations. Even in 1934 when the income from fishing was at its nadir of only $23,230, this sum represented 42 per cent of the total income for that year. In 1920, when the income from fishing was at its alltime peak of $182,500, this sum represented 71 per cent of the total Kwakiutl earnings for the year.

The amount of earnings from hunting remained small and relatively constant in comparison with the other categories of earnings, although the total did decrease gradually throughout the period. At no time was it an important percentage of Kwakiutl yearly income.

No figures except those for direct earnings from their own labor are given until 1918, when we see the entry of $120 for land and timber rents. From 1918 through 1939 there are widely varying amounts coming from timber rents, with a high point in 1923 of $14,736. However, even this amount represents merely seven per cent of the total Kwakiutl income for that year. The next largest income from timber rent, $14,089 in 1938, again represents only eight per cent of total Kwakiutl income for the year. Land rents provide an insignificant amount from 1923 on. Annuties, which appear first in the table in 1922, never reach an amount large enough to figure significantly in total income. The largest income received from this source was $4,167 in the year 1939.

The table as a whole indicates the degree to which the Kwakiutl were economically self-supporting and independent. Throughout the years 1903–1921 the annual per capita income of the Kwakiutl increased. From 1903 through 1939 it was primarily a money income rather than an income in kind, and an earned income rather than one derived from windfalls of rents, interest, governmental appropriations or other unearned sources. This direct evidence gives additional support to the picture of the Kwakiutl economy as healthy, vigorous and ongoing.

It is supported and extended by the indirect evidence. From 1903 to 1932 there is a large and cumulative increase in the value of Kwakiutl real and personal property. The valuation placed on real and personal property in 1928, $676,218, represents approximately a sixfold increase over the lowest valuation, $117,538, in 1903. Even in the depression the valuation remains at $577,670 for 1932, approximately a five-fold increase over the 1903 low. Figure 1 shows the increase in the value of real and personal property over these years.

According to the same agency reports on which the previous figures are based, the value of private dwellings is seen to increase steeply and continuously from 1908 to 1928, the period for which these figures are available. This increase is somewhat surprising in view of the fact that during these years the Kwakiutl population was declining. It is also true that during this period the number of large, communal, old-style dwellings remained relatively constant until the year 1920, when the agency figures indicate a sharp decrease lasting until 1929. It is possible that the valuation given by the agents to "private dwellings" represents primarily the relatively few and unimportant single-family dwelling units which the agent saw as symbols of progress and decency. Whether, then, this increased valuation of private dwellings is very important when most of the Kwakiutl population is still living in the communal type of dwelling, is uncertain. It is, however, certain that here again there is evidence of increasing money income and wealth. Cash was required for the building and furnishing of private dwellings. Even as early as 1883 one Kwakiutl man is described as returning from a profitable season in the hop fields of the south with purchases which included windows, doors and nails, a clock and a mirror. Twenty-five years later, although admitting that the prevailing type of house was still the "huge barn-like structure," the Kwakiutl agent describes a chief as having "a neat little cottage, well painted and furnished. He has inlaid linoleum on the floor, pictures on the wall, all neatly framed ..." The Superintendent General of Indian Affairs mentions that throughout British Columbia the money earned by Indians during the prosperity of the First World War was very largely put either into the purchase or manufacture of launches, or into the improvement of their homes. The prosperity of the Second World War years was likewise reflected in Indian dwellings in this area. The 1941 report states that the "high standards of comfort and decor exhibited is quite remarkable, kitchen and bathrooms being equipped with most modern conveniences."[85] Compared to the corresponding figures for the United States the increase among the Kwakiutl of the value of real and personal property and the value of private dwellings is much greater (Fig. 3).

Further evidence as to the increasing cash income of the Kwakiutl may be found in the general increase in the prices of the items which they produced and sold. This evidence is impressive in spite of its incompleteness. One of the earliest reports on prices concerns the Hudson's Bay Company post, Fort Rupert, in the center of Kwakiutl territory. Mayne gives a series of prices for furs and profits to the Company from their dealings with the Kwakiutl, beginning with 1859. The trade blanket at that time was worth $1.57 in United States money, if the pound sterling is taken as $4.84. Mayne gives 500 "minx" skins as being traded at the rate of 30 per trade blanket, which would mean that the price paid to the Indians was slightly more than five cents per skin.[86] About twenty years later, according to the chronology given by Ford

[85] *Ibid.*, 1883, p. 48; 1910, p. 236; 1918, p. 38; 1941, p. 179.
[86] Mayne, 1862, p. 185.

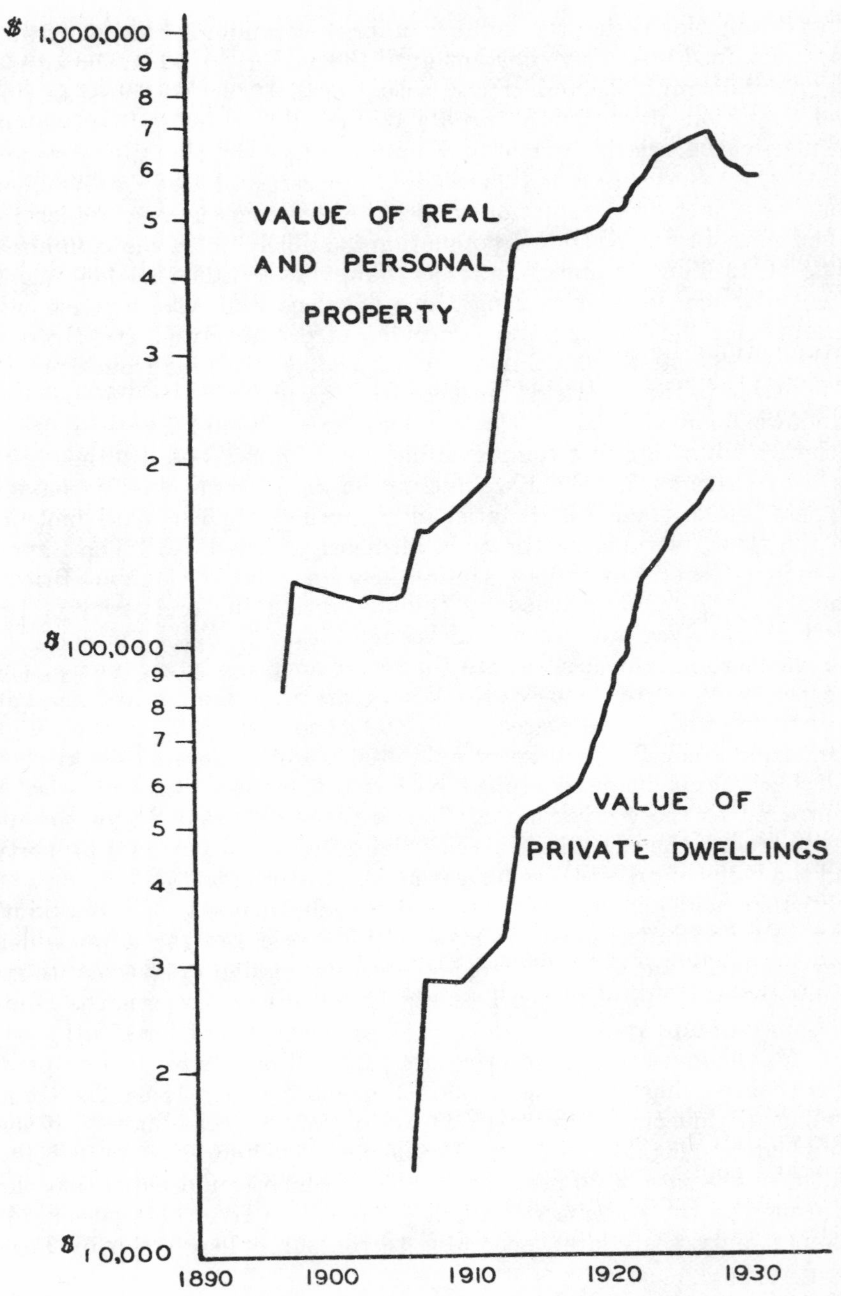

Fig. 3. Increase in the Value of Real and Personal Property and in the Value of Private Dwellings (based on data in Canada, Annual Reports of Indian Affairs). *Ratio scale.*

(it is not possible to fix the date precisely) and on the basis of the internal evidence in the autobiography, *Smoke from their Fires*, a small mink skin seems to have brought ten cents, or nearly double the earlier price.[87]

The price of halibut, another important product of Kwakiutl economic activity, also showed a marked increase.[88] In 1890 they received one dollar for 100 pieces of halibut; by 1905 they were receiving one dollar for only thirty pieces, and by 1910, for twenty pieces. This represents a five-fold increase. Curtis enlarges on this information by saying that halibut had been known to sell for as high as four pieces to the dollar, but he does not give the date at which this price occurred.

There is evidence also of increases in the prices of certain goods manufactured by the Kwakiutl which were objects of internal trade. In this case the price is quoted in terms of pairs of blankets although this need not be taken as more than the traditional way of estimating value. The Kwakiutl were always able to convert money prices into blankets, or blanket prices into money or other items. The dates in this case are not exact, but there seems to have been an increase of ten to twenty-fold in the price of canoes within the memory of the narrator.

> . . . The Blunden Harbor, the Newette, and Smith's Inlet Indians came to Fort Rupert to sell their canoes. We made some at Fort Rupert, but not so many. We'd buy our paddles mostly from the Blunden Harbor Indians. They are made of yew. We paid for a small canoe, five pairs of blankets; maybe two pairs of blankets for a very small canoe. A real canoe was ten to twenty pairs. You couldn't get a canoe now for less than two hundred pairs.[89]

All of this evidence must be considered in the context of the growth of the money economy in the midst of which the Kwakiutl were functioning and with which they had many profitable connections. British Columbia was undergoing an enormous industrial expansion in these years, whether measured by the value of its fish products, the price of salmon, or the value of its fisheries. It is not surprising, in view of the Kwakiutl occupational and financial situation, to see them benefiting from the expansion of the British Columbia economy as it became more and more integrated with world monetary economy.

Population

During most of its recorded history and throughout the years when the Kwakiutl were making a success out of their new economic situation, Kwakiutl population shows a rapid and continuous decline. It is surprising that a people who seem to be dying out should retain such vigor as they had in the economic matters which have been described and in

[87] Ford, 1941, p. 96.
[88] Curtis, 1915, pp. 26—29.
[89] Ford, 1941, p. 75.

their social and ceremonial life, and especially their potlatching, which will be described and discussed below. The decline of Kwakiutl population was not arrested until 1924. At this turning point the first increase in Kwakiutl population history was recorded and, since the decline of the population had been brought about primarily by disease, the reversal of this morbid trend seems to have been due to increased medical care and possibly to the development of immunities to the infectious and contagious diseases introduced by Europeans with devastating consequences.

The earliest estimate of Kwakiutl population is that of John Work in his census of 1836—1841.[90] His figures give a total of 23,587, omitting five groups with a population of 4,105 as not certainly Kwakiutl. The reliability of Work's figures can be questioned also on other grounds, since his totals in almost every case are mere multiples of the number of houses in a village and the number of inhabitants in a house. He estimates forty-nine inhabitants per house for villages of forty or fifty houses in six out of seven cases, and sixty-two or sixty-four inhabitants per house for villages of thirty houses in seven out of eight cases. These figures seem excessive and arbitrary. Another reason for suspecting that Work's figure is too high is that ten years later in 1883 the Kwakiutl agent gave a total population of only 2,264 which would indicate a decline of ninety per cent in less than half a century.

However, it may be that the figure given for 1883 was too low. Boas questioned the reliability of the agency returns for 1883, 1884 and 1885 on the grounds that in those years the census was taken at a time when the people were scattered to their fishing stations.[91] Moreover, inspection of the returns reveal impossibly abrupt increases in the population of several very small Kwakiutl villages.

Another difficulty with the Kwakiutl agency returns is that they were made for each of the various Kwakiutl sub-groups, such as Nimkish, Koskimo, Mamaleleqala and Matilpi. These sub-groups were further divided into numayms which were the fundamental units in the consciousness of the people.[92] Individuals often had positions in two numayms. The numayms, and even the sub-groups, are known in historical times to have moved from certain localities and amalgamated with other numayms and sub-groups. Dawson reports, for instance, that after the establishment of Fort Rupert by the Hudson's Bay Company in 1849 people from the villages of Klik-si-wi at the mouth of a river of the same name, of Ka-loo-kwis on Turnour Island, Whulk at Alert Bay, and White Beach on Harbledown Island, came to settle at the Fort and formed the sub-groups of Kwa-ki-ool, Walis-Kwa-kiool and Kwi-ha.[93]

[90] Curtis, 1915, p. 303.
[91] Boas, 1887, p. 230.
[92] Boas, 1920, p. 11.
[93] Dawson, 1887, pp. 10f.

There were other such amalgamations and resettlements of the Kwakiutl. Several of them seem to have been a consequence of the reduction of Kwakiutl population in the historical period.[94]

With facts of such intricacy, the agent's figures for any one sub-group might well be unreliable. The same factors would not, however, operate to the same degree to make the census figure for the total Kwakiutl population unreliable. The total figures clearly show a continuous steep decline in Kwakiutl population from 1883 to 1924.

The principal cause of this decline was disease. Relatively few deaths were ascribed by the historical sources to violence or accident, but there is an extensive record of diseases that killed and diseases that destroyed fertility. Although the Kwakiutl seem to have had no direct contact with Europeans or Americans until the circumnavigation of Vancouver Island by Vancouver in 1792, they may have been indirectly exposed to the new diseases from the time of the arrival of Cook in Nootka Sound in 1778. More than 140 British and American ships were trading to the Northwest Coast between the years 1785 and 1815[95] and contact among the various Indian groups of the coast in trade, warfare and slave-taking would certainly have been sufficient to spread the imported diseases.

Unfortunately, the details of Kwakiutl health are not recorded until 1837. James Douglas in the Fort Vancouver Letters says that the year 1837 "was marked by the frightful progress of the Small Pox among the Native Tribes."[96] Since his letter continues with a discussion of trade in Queen Charlotte's Sound and the adjacent harbors and the traffic of the "Native Coquilt Pedlers," it is clear that the Kwakiutl were affected.

No further information is available until nearly a generation later. Sometime between 1874 and 1876 Brabant, a missionary in the area, tells of burying victims of smallpox.[97] The Indian Affairs report for 1876

[94] Boas, 1920, p. 111: "One of the greatest obstacles to a clear understanding of the social organization of the Kwakiutl is the general confusion caused by the reduction in numbers of the tribe . . . There is a very fundamental difficulty in the definition of the tribal unit and of its subdivisions. I do not know of a single Kwakiutl tribe that is at present an undivided unit. All those studied consist of well-recognized subdivisions.

"Furthermore, a single locality is claimed as the place of origin of each division of the tribe. In the consciousness of the people these divisions are fundamental units. The development of the concept of a tribal unit is not, by any means clear, except in so far as it appears as an effect of the congregation in one place of a number of local units. Recent tradition, the historical truth of which cannot well be doubted, shows clearly that such a congregation has occurred repeatedly. Units may also have broken up, owing to inner dissensions or to other accidents."

[95] Howay, Sage, and Angus, 1942, p. 16.

[96] Rich, 1941, p. 244.

[97] Brabant, 1900, p. 24.

TABLE 11

Kwakiutl Population through 1934

Year	Population	Diseases Noted	Source
Pre-Contact	17,300		Kroeber (1934) estimate of central maritime pop. including Bella Coola
1836—41	23,586		John Work's estimate, in Curtis, 1915
1837		Smallpox	James Douglas
1853	about 7,000		Hall, 1888
1872	3,500		Canada. Annual Report Indian Affairs
1876		Smallpox	Ibid.
1877	3,000	Smallpox	Ibid.
1880	2,500		Ibid.
1881		Measles, V.D., T.B.	Ibid.
1882	2,264	Measles, V.D.	Boas, 1887
1883	2,264	Measles	Ibid.
1884	1,889		Ibid.
1885	1,969		Dawson, 1887
1887		V.D.	Canada. Annual Report Indian Affairs
1889	1,898	V.D.	Ibid.
1890	1,797	Influenza	Ibid.
1891	1,732	Influenza	Ibid.
1892	1,678	Influenza	Ibid.
1896	1,639		Ibid.
1897	1,605		Ibid.
1898	1,597		Ibid.
1903	1,345	T.B., Pneumonia, Bronchitis	Ibid.
1904	1,317		Ibid.
1905	1,278		Ibid.
1906	1,257		Ibid.
1907	1,305		Ibid.
1908	1,294	Measles	Ibid.
1909	1,263		Ibid.
1910	1,238		Ibid.
1911	1,208		Ibid.
1912	1,199		Ibid.
1913	1,183		Ibid.
1914	1,183		Ibid.
1917	1,134		Ibid.
1924	1,039	T. B.	Ibid.
1928	1,088		Ibid.
1934	1,173		Ibid.

confirms the existence of an epidemic, stating, "In each of the Superintendencies of the Province the expense incurred for medicines, medical attendance, etc., has been very considerable, owing to the prevalence of smallpox amongst the Indians. In the Victoria Superintendency, the items on the account amount to $3,114.20."[98] The following year the disease was still sufficiently prevalent to cause expenses of over $2,500.[99] I. W. Powell, the Superintendent in Victoria, writes in 1876 that 900 Indians were vaccinated and that the smallpox was confined altogether to the northern Indians who were permitted to reside in Victoria.[100]

Since Indians in large numbers, including the Kwakiutl, were attracted to Victoria for a variety of reasons, it was one of the chief centers for the spread of infectious diseases among them. Boas describes the slum conditions which existed in the Indian section of Victoria about this time:

> The streets are lined with poor little huts which house the Indians who are temporarily in Victoria. The smallest of these huts are sheds of boards divided into rooms by wooden partitions. In each room a rough bed and a hearth are installed and it is ready to rent for about two dollars a month. Such a wooden shack, twenty feet wide by sixty feet long, therefore brings the owner two hundred dollars a year and, since this income is gained practically without any initial expenditure, a great number of landlords have turned over their property to such use. In these huts the Indians who are in Victoria as temporary laborers live, often with their wives and children; in them also live Indian women who earn money as washerwomen or prostitutes and who plan to return to their homes with their savings.[101]

Powell protests in 1877: "It is pitiable to hear of such cities as Victoria and New Westminster objecting to bear the expenses of caring for the Indians attacked with diseases of an infectious type within their precincts."[102]

Evidence of extremely poor health in many sections of the Kwakiutl population is given by George Blenkinsop, the Kwakiutl agent, in 1881. In that year there were thirty-seven cases of illness among the Koskimo, and twelve deaths to only three births.[103] Since the population of the Koskimo two years later was given as 192,[104] some idea of the 1881 death and birth rates can be obtained. In another instance he states:

> On landing at the Nah-kwock-to village, seeing quite a number of apparently healthy children playing on the beach and sporting in the water, it appeared at first sight that there was one spot in the Agency where the natives were free from the contamination of those fearful diseases which

[98] Canada. Annual Report on Indian Affairs, 1876, p. 47.
[99] *Ibid.*, Return C (4).
[100] *Ibid.*, p. 35.
[101] Boas, 1891a, p. 76. Translated by the writer.
[102] Canada. Annual Report on Indian Affairs, 1877, p. 16.
[103] *Ibid.*, 1881, p. 169.
[104] Boas, 1887, p. 230.

have been and now are so rapidly decimating most of the tribes on the coast, but I was quickly undeceived.

Upwards of 20 of these children were in an unhealthy condition, and several others within doors, of a tender age, required medical attendance. Several, young as they were, had scrofula in its worst form, two or three were spitting blood, and the constant cough, heard in all directions, told but too plainly that consumption was doing its work. In all there were 52 cases of sickness in this village.[105]

Blenkinsop mentions an "unprecendented amount of illness" in 1882. In 1883, measles caused the death of sixty-eight children, mortality being the highest among the Nimkish. Two cases of smallpox in the agency did not however result in an epidemic because of the vaccination measures which had been taken. In 1885 the health of the tribes was reported as good "with the exception of the Nah-kwock-toes, who are much subjected to scrofula occasioned by non-intermarriage with neighbors [sic]."

In 1891 and 1892 the succeeding agent, Pidcock, tells of an influenza epidemic which attacked half the Indians in the agency and carried off about seventy of the older people. In 1903 Agent G. W. DeBeck mentions consumption as the most prevalent disease, and in the following year he notes poor general health, and the presence of pneumonia, bronchititis and consumption. In 1908 Agent Halliday mentions a bad epidemic of measles.

A committee of experts under the auspices of the Canada Tuberculosis Association made a survey for the department of Indian Affairs in 1926–27 of the prevalence of tuberculosis among the Indians of British Columbia. They found that tuberculosis was about five times more common among the Indians than among the general population.[106]

In addition to being unusually subject to respiratory infections, the Indians were especially susceptible to veneral diseases, described in the agency reports as "those fearful diseases," "scrofula," or "scrofula in its worst form." These diseases were not only a direct cause of death but also contributed to the low birthrate and the high infant and child mortality. It is apparent from Table 12 that the decline in the Kwakiutl population was due not only to continual losses, but also to a lack of any healthy capacity to replace those losses.

Closely associated with veneral disease as a factor in the declining birthrate was the prevalence of prostitution among the Indian women, after the arrival of Europeans in that area. Menzies in 1792 had reported on the Nimkish women of Alert Bay in relation to European men,

105 Canada. Annual Report on Indian Affairs, 1881, pp. 169—70. Blenkinsop's first census of the Nah-kwock-to, in 1883, numbers them at 167. This figure is to be found in the Boas reference cited above.

106 Canada. Annual Report on Indian Affairs, 1882, p. 66; 1883, p. 47; 1885, p. 84; 1891, p. 119; 1892, p. 236; 1903, p. 291; 1904, p. 5; 1908, p. 243; 1928, pp. 7–8.

"... tho they were free and unreserved in their manners and conversation, yet none of them would suffer any of our people to offer them any indecent familiarities, which is a modesty in some measure characteristic of their tribe."[107] Whatever the reasons for the unavailability of Kwakiutl women at this time, the situation had changed markedly by the time the agency period began in 1872. It seems likely that the prostitution of Kwakiutl women began with the British Columbia gold rush of 1858, when twenty-five to thirty thousand American men set out for the Fraser River and made Victoria their starting point and supply center.[108] There is no doubt that the Kwakiutl had the misfortune to come into contact with carriers of veneral disease from a culture which sanctioned prostitution and made it an economically profitable employment.

Again and again the reports of the agents refer to the danger to the health of the Indians from the influx of so many single men into the mines, fisheries, logging camps and other occupations in the frontier days. In 1881 Blenkinsop mentions "the haunts of vice at Victoria and Burrard Inlet" and comments on the exceptional good health of the Kingcombe Inlet group: "These Indians keep almost entirely to themselves. ... Few, if any, go to Victoria ... they are, therefore, free from many of the diseases which other coast tribes are subject to." In 1887 Pidcock, the succeeding agent, says: "Generally the health of the different bands has been good, but the number of those afflicted with scrofula in its worst form is very numerous." In 1890 he comments that "The logging camps in the neighborhood (of the Kwakiutl of Cape Mudge), while affording employment, are a great snare."[109]

Kwakiutl women were the first group in the population to be infected with veneral disease, and the group from which the infection spread to the rest. Boas, writing sometime before 1891, expresses great concern for the future of the Indians of the region and especially for the Kwakiutl of Fort Rupert because of the prostitution of Indian women in Victoria:

> This custom has been very destructive for many of the coastal tribes, since they lose almost all their young women. The tribes of Ft. Rupert have in this way been brought almost to extinction. All the measures taken so far to put an end to this pernicious practice have been fruitless and even the most remote tribes today send their daughters to Victoria to certain destruction.[110]

Halliday, the agent in 1907, claims that the Klawatsis and Matilpi had ceased prostituting their women at logging camps, and that to a large extent this same practice had ceased among the Wewaiaikum and

[107] Newcombe, 1923, p. 87.

[108] Howay, Sage, and Angus, 1942.

[109] Canada. Annual Report on Indian Affairs, 1881, p. 171; 1885, p. 84; 1887, p. 109; 1890, p. 76.

[110] Boas, 1891a, p. 76. Translated by the writer.

Kwiahkah of the vicinity of Cape Mudge, but he adds that "they are still paying for their former sins." Two years later he reports for the Kwakiutl as a whole that "prostitution is rife among them."[111]

The data are not sufficiently precise to indicate the extent to which venereal disease contributed to the decline in the Kwakiutl population, or to permit any very clear separation of its effects from those of the other diseases to which the Kwakiutl were subjected as a result of their contact with Americans and Europeans. But it is clear that venereal disease and prostitution together were an important factor in the failure of the Kwakiutl to maintain their numbers.

The number of women throughout the historical period is consistently smaller than the number of men, in the age groups 16–20 years and 21–65 years, which include the whole childbearing period with the possible exception of the girls of fourteen and fifteen years. In 1888 the agent complains that "the scarcity of wives for young men is a draw back" to the progress of the Kwakiutl, and in 1892 he notes that the census again showed a decline of the Kwakiutl and that "only a few are likely to become mothers."[112] Boas relates the story of three young sisters who went with their parents to Victoria and spent the winter as prostitutes; their return to Fort Rupert with the wealth they had earned was shortly followed by the illness and death of all three.[113] It is highly probable that venereal disease was at least a contributing cause.

It is also possible of course that the Kwakiutl population was losing women who went off as prostitutes or as wives to white men, and never returned to their home villages, although there is no indication of such occurrences in the sources.

Personal and housekeeping habits of the Kwakiutl as depicted in the literature seem to have been cleanly. Their living quarters were roomy and uncrowded, and they had an uncontaminated supply of drinking water. In 1889 the agent reported that

> . . . as a whole they still live in their primitive houses, large buildings made from rough cedar boards. Still, in almost every village there are some small frame houses, often very carefully and cleanly kept, but it is doubtful if they are as healthy in some respects as the old houses, as the Indians huddle in them for warmth in the cold weather, and they become unbearably hot.[114]

In spite of this, the agents waged a continuous war against the standard "great house" of the Kwakiutl, "the large and filthy rancheries,"[115] a campaign carried on (unsuccessfully) as much in the name of

[111] Canada. Annual Report on Indian Affairs, 1907, pp. 239, 246.

[112] *Ibid.*, 1888, p. 104; 1892, p. 236. Table 12 is compiled from tbe same source 1897–1934.

[113] Boas, 1925, pp. 93–94.

[114] Canada. Annual Report on Indian Affairs, 1889, p. 256.

[115] *Ibid.*, 1876, p. 34 (Powell).

TABLE 12

Composition of Kwakiutl Population (1897—1934)

Year	Total	Under 6 M	Under 6 F	6–15 M	6–15 F	16–20 M	16–20 F	21–65 M	21–65 F	Over 65 M	Over 65 F
1897	1605	117	94	95	75	76	61	533	508	28	18
1898	1597	100	97	98	86	76	64	533	513	18	12
1899	1554	102	106	92	82	59	52	533	505	17	6
1904	1317	89	75	80	67	57	19	458	377	42	53
1905	1278	84	71	72	63	51	14	470	379	32	42
1906	1257	79	73	73	62	51	15	466	378	25	35
1907	1305	72	69	110	77	42	23	455	400	21	36
1908	1294	71	64	114	80	43	21	448	398	23	32
1910	1238	90	103	107	69	29	25	422	344	25	34
1911	1208	99	87	115	73	29	20	400	338	20	27
1912	1199	98	90	115	70	33	16	382	338	25	32
1913	1186	97	90	111	68	33	19	384	338	22	24
1914	1183	80	73	108	90	31	15	384	340	26	36
1924	1039	63	73	113	101	35	30	304	272	27	21
1928	1088	81	80	127	121	48	50	286	228	37	30
		Under 7		7–16		17–21		22–65			
1934	1173	156	114	136	134	42	40	266	225	32	28

developing progress in individuality and of discouraging winter dances and potlatch gatherings, as in the name of health. The Indians never built more than a few of the European single family houses advocated by the agents.

Although in one case the agent Blenkinsop told the Noo-we-te "to keep clean," without specifying the method,[116] the Indian sanitary practices seem to have been good for that period, and possibly better than those of the nearby towns. The agents warned the Indians to stay away from such places as Victoria on grounds of health as well as of vice.[117] The slums of Victoria would certainly be worse than any pre-contact living conditions. Nor could anything the Indians might do in the way of the mishandling of food be worse than the actions of the missionary Brabant in feeding the Indians molasses out of which he had just fished two dozen drowned mice.[118] European and American immigrants brought them no new safeguards against the new infections.

[116] *Ibid.*, 1881, p. 168.

[117] *Ibid.*, 1881, p. 169.

[118] Rev. A. J. Brabant, 1867, p. 53. It was Brabant also who enlisted the help of the Indians in burying victims of the smallpox by offering them a concoction of boiled water, biscuits and sugar with the assurance that it "would be the best preservative in the world against small-pox" (p. 24).

Boas says of the Indian prospects, in what he terms their *Weltkämpfe* with the Whites:

> If their hygienic practices are improved so that the terrible infant mortality is reduced and if the efforts of the Canadian government to make them independent producers are successful, then we may hope that the sad spectacle of the complete destruction of these richly endowed peoples can be avoided.[119]

He is certainly correct in stating that improved hygiene was in order, and that it would help to minimize the decline in population, but it is doubtful whether improved hygiene alone could turn a population trend.

As remedies for the ills to which they were subject, the Kwakiutl possessed an extensive pharmacopoeia of purgatives, emetics, diuretics, poultices, infusions for diarrhoea, and pain killers. They had also some elaborate methods of treatment for specific ailments, including a complicated method of relieving the pain of boils and carbuncles, and an imaginative and undoubtedly successful treatment for severe and extensive burns by placing the patient inside the blubbery skin of a seal.

When herb remedies were to be used, the husband, wife or brother of the patient would collect the plant, prepare it, and treat the patient with it. At the same time he (or she) would say a prayer in the form of a statement that he hoped the treatment would be effective, and that the patient would be cured or relieved. In all of this there was no real involvement of the supernatural. If the treatment proved ineffectice, or if the patient had an extraordinary complaint, the shaman might be called in. However the shamans seem to have been generally regarded by the Kwakiutl as fakers rather than as healers; if their ministrations did prove to be effective it was assumed that they were sorcerers of malign power and intent.

The attitude of the Kwakiutl, by present standards, was fairly realistic. Although they feared death by sorcery they did not live in a world in which health was constantly menaced or restored by supernatural means.[120] And when additional medicines and treatments were made available to them they were prepared to accept them and did accept them readily.[121] There seems never to have been any reluctance to use vaccination against smallpox, and at no time do the Indian agents record any unwillingness in Kwakiutl territory to accept medicines or go to hospitals. Although there is no actual record of it, it seems possible that the Kwakiutl, like the Indians of the northern coast, may have "incontinently dose(d) themselves with all sorts of patent medicines which they (bought) . . . from the traders."[122]

[119] Boas, 1889, p. 12. Translated by the writer.
[120] Boas, 1930, pp. 1–53, 209–245.
[121] Canada. Annual Report on Indian Affairs, 1876, p. 35.
[122] Niblack, 1888.

Although the Kwakiutl were quite ready to accept anything offered to them in the form of medical care and were obviously in great need of health services, the record of the agencies indicates that very little was done for them in this respect. The distribution of medicines by the agent seems to have been the sole medical attention received by them for many years. This was probably in line with the practice of the Hudson's Bay officers, since there is a record of such activity on their part in other sections of the Northwest Coast. The financial reports of the Victoria superintendency between 1872 and 1880 contain items for medicines some of which may have gone to the Kwakiutl. Beginning in 1880, the financial returns of the "Kwakewlth" agency list medicines for the Indians, rent of dispensary, light and fuel for dispensary, attendance and board of a sick Indian at the Royal Hospital, six days' hospital attendance and medicine at the St. Joseph's Hospital in Victoria, treatment of Indians at the St. Paul's Hospital of Vancouver, medical attendance, maintenance and care of a patient at the Public Hospital for the Insane. The first of the items for hospital care does not appear until 1890. Items for medicine which it is likely that the agent himself dispensed continue through 1907, and perhaps beyond that, although the form of financial return after that year obscure the details of medical and hospital expenditures.

"Up to the present time no medical man had been connected in any way with the agency," writes Halliday in 1909, "the only doctor being the resident doctor at Queen's Hospital at Rock Bay; but as the hospital was not equipped to handle patients, none of them went there except in great emergency." In 1909 a hospital was built in Alert Bay, with "separate wards for Indian patients, who will receive exactly the same treatment as white patients." Several years later a hospital was built at Campbell River.[123]

The bulk of the money appropriated for agency expenses went always to the salaries and living and travelling expenses of the agent, until the most recent years. However, of the money actually spent on the Indians, the medical and hospital expenditures made up the largest part. Even so, the amounts were strikingly inadequate. The per capita health expenditures of the agency in 1880 were less than one-half of one cent. It was not until 1889 that they reached the figure of ten cents per capita per year. By 1914 they had risen to more than one dollar per capita per year, and in 1924 they jumped suddenly to more than nine dollars per capita (see Table 13).

Sometime between 1924 and 1928 the decline of Kwakiutl population was arrested. Since disease had been the principal cause of the population decline, the factors contributing to Kwakiutl health were what

[123] Canada. Annual Report on Indian Affairs, 1909, p. 245.

finally arrested and reversed the downward trend. Among these medical care was probably the most important. Kwakiutl ideas, health practices and sanitation were not of a nature to interfere seriously with the effectiveness of any medical care made available to them and the turning point in the population trend was consequent on a real increase in per capita medical expenditures. Another factor of possible equal or greater importance, but one difficult to establish or measure, was the gradual immunization of the population against the new diseases that had been brought to them. Influenza, measles and whooping cough were at first fatal killers and at the time there were no preventive measures against

TABLE 13[124]

Medical and Hospital Expenditures of Kwakiutl Agency (1822—1924)

Date	Pop.	Medical and Hospital Expenditure	Per Capita M. & H. Expenditure	M. & H. Expenditure, per cent of Total Expenditure of Kwakiutl Agency
1880	2,500	$ 10.12	$ 00.004	
1882	2,264	190.74	00.081	9 %
1883	2,264	163.38	00.071	8 %
1885	1,969	96.52	00.058	5 %
1886	1,969	84.50	00.042	8 %
1887	1,969	6.50	00.003	4 %
1888	1,969	53.88	00.027	2 %
1889	1,898	211.43	00.116	12 %
1890	1,797	353.84	00.196	14 %
1904–5	1,317	270.92	00.205	7 %
1905–6	1,278	530.84	00.415	12 %
1906–7	1,257	408.81	00.324	11 %
1914–5	1,183	3942.20[125]	3.33	46 %
1915–6	1,183	2109.50	1.78	35 %
1916–7	1,134	3034.55	2.67	42 %
1917–8	1,134	1461.90	1.29	21 %
1918–19	1,134	2185.69	1.92	25 %
1919–20	1,134	2442.92	2.15	33 %
1920–21	1,134	3170.75	2.79	32 %
1924	1,039	9484.00	9.11	50 %

[124] Compiled from the Financial Statements in the Annual Reports of Indian Affairs of Canada. Responsibility for the computation of the per capita Medical and Hospital Expenditures and the per cent of Total Agency Expenditure made by the Medical and Hospital Expenditure rests with the author. Figures for Medical and Hospital Expenditure before 1905–6 are totals made by the author of the relevant items in the itemized financial statements. After that time totals are to be found in the financial reports and as "Medical and Hospital Expenditure."

[125] This item includes a grant for the construction of a hospital at Campbell River.

them as there were against smallpox. In later years these diseases do not seem to figure importantly in mortality and it seems reasonable to assume that they were no longer deadly to the population. Further factors contributing to Kwakiutl health can be found in changes in the conditions of the European settlements in the area. Disordered boom towns gradually became stable communities and the increase in public health measures and the decrease in prostitution made the new cities and towns far safer for the Indians.

The decline of Kwakiutl population from before 1850 until 1924 did not have the disruptive effects on the culture that might have been expected. The description of various aspects of Kwakiutl economic life shows continuous vitality and remarkable success in adjusting to the new conditions and even in exploiting them. The description and analysis of Kwakiutl social structure, rivalry and potlatching will show that the population decline exaggerated certain tendencies already present in Kwakiutl life. There is evidence particularly that it stimulated potlatching, a fact that had far reaching effects upon the historical development of Kwakiutl culture. These changes, as will be seen, can not be called weakening or disruptive. Rather the population decline, contrary to the usual and reasonable expectation, seems actually to have contributed toward Kwakiutl success in maintaining cultural identity.

CHAPTER THREE

THE KWAKIUTL POTLATCH

There were both continuities and changes in the Kwakiutl potlatch during the period for which historical data exist. Since the Kwakiutl potlatch was described early and in great detail by Boas, it has often been taken as the classic type of the Northwest Coast culture area. So true is this that the uniqueness of specifically Kwakiutl characteristics have been lost in the process.[1] Various authors have shown how different from the Kwakiutl potlatch was that, for example, of the Haida,[2] the Tsmishian[3] and the Coast Salish.[4] It is equally valid to assert that these

[1] Although Ruth Benedict states in *Patterns of Culture* (1934, p. 175) that her description applies almost wholly to Kwakiutl, she heads this section of her book "The Northwest Coast of America" and she uses this name in cases where her examples are drawn wholly from Kwakiutl. Since her book is, for the general reader as well as the social scientist, it is only in the specialized study that exception could be taken to the impression given. A far more serious case of discussing the Kwakiutl potlatch as though it were the form of an institution typical of an entire area can be found in Moret and Davy *From Tribe to Empire*, (1926). Here, as the title suggests, the authors formulate an evolutionary sequence. A major division of this sequence is the "Progressive Concentration of Power in Primitive Societies," under which we find *the* "Potlatch" discussed as one of the "conditions of the individualization of power." When the authors do not depend entirely upon Kwakiutl data, they lump Haida, Tlingit, Tsimshian and Kwakiutl data indiscriminately together.

[2] Murdock, 1936, pp. 20ff. Murdock describes and analyzes the potlatch of the Haida of Masset. His conclusion is that "The potlatch is discovered to be the dynamic factor in the most vital of all native institutions – the system of rank and status." While this element is present in the Kwakiutl potlatch, no published analysis of it has failed to include several other factors as at least equally vital.

[3] Garfield, 1939, pp. 167–340. The description of the Tsimshian potlatch makes it clear that the primary feature is the giving of a series of lavish feasts. Again potlatching in Kwakiutl included the giving of feasts, but the potlatching distribution was of blankets or other articles of native or white manufacture. Many other differences could be pointed out.

[4] Barnett (1938, pp. 349–358) brings out clearly that the feature present in the potlatch of the entire area including Kwakiutl is that it is ". . a congregation of people, ceremoniously and often individually invited to witness a demonstration of family prerogative" and that since these witnesses are judges as well as spectators of the potlatch drama, the result is the greatest possible public effectiveness and social participation. At the same time he asserts that the contest element present in Kwakiutl is abnormal from an areal point of view.

studies affirm the uniqueness of the Kwakiutl potlatch. It is important to underline this point because the present study does not deal with the potlatch as an abstract institution in this area but with the Kwakiutl potlatch in relation to relevant and specific Kwakiutl history.

The Kwakiutl potlatch is the ostentatious and dramatic distribution of property by the holder of a fixed, ranked and named social position, to other position holders. The purpose is to validate the hereditary claim to the position and to live up to it by maintaining its relative glory and rank against the rivalrous claims of the others. There did not need to be any special occasion for giving a potlatch, or the occasion could be merely nominal. Potlatches were always given, however, on the occasion of the numerous changes of name from birth to child's name to young man's name to potlatch name, on marriages, and the birth of children to the married couple, and on initiations into the secret societies of the winter dance ceremonial.

"Potlatching" is, however, more than any single potlatch. The public distribution of property by an individual is a recurrent climax in an endless series of cycles of accumulating property – distributing it in a potlatch – being given property – again accumulating and preparing. The whole potlatch system is a composition of these numerous individual potlatch cycles and is supported and maximized in Kwakiutl by certain social and economic features, the details of which clarify this general definition.

The first of these features is that potlatching existed in the context of a fantastic[5] surplus economy. It would not be accurate to make the distinction between a prestige and a subsistence economy for the Kwakiutl as Cora DuBois has done for another Northwest Coast group, because in Kwakiutl, unlike Tolowa-Tututni,[6] there is not one kind of property for subsistence requirements and another for prestige. The main concern was for quantity and some subsistence items were accumulated in fantastic surpluses above any conceivable need and served as the appropriate counters for potlatching. Chief among quantity items were Hudson's Bay trade blankets priced at 50 cents for a single one, $1.50 for a double one. In pre-contact times there had been blankets of

He denies that the capital investment or loaning aspect of potlatching is present anywhere, including Kwakiutl. It is difficult to see how this is possible as the text will make clear. Rather the investment feature should have been considered as a special Kwakiutl development. This study is very valuable in that it does point up some basic features of the potlatches of all the cultures in this area. It stretches the point, however, to deny the existence of special features in the cultures of the area or to label them as "abnormal."

[5] Bunzel, 1938. This is the word used in describing this part of Kwakiutl economic life (p. 359).

[6] DuBois, 1936, pp. 49–65.

cedar bark or various kinds of furs sewn together. Perhaps of second importance were canoes of native manufacture. Other items called "trifles," literally "bad things,"[7] names which indicate their relative lack of prestige in potlatching, included a large list of goods which in recent times have been mostly of modern industrial manufacture: flour, silk scarfs, lengths of dress goods, zinc wash boilers, sewing machines, phonographs, brass bracelets, kettles, dishes, pails, or even Canadian money. In olden times they were entirely articles of native produce or manufacture: deer or other dressed animal skins, mats, baskets, boxes of oil, and spoons of mountain goat horn. These articles were not "treasures," like the Tolowa-Tututni woodpecker scalps or wonderful obsidian blades; rather they were all potentially useful everyday objects which, however, were acquired in such enormous quantities that their relation to the useful and everyday approached a vanishing point. They were also acquired originally by the same economic methods as those which assured ordinary livelihood. It is, of course, impossible to say whether the exuberant industriousness and inventiveness of the Kwakiutl were causes or results of the desire to acquire surpluses.

Secondly, individuals who took part in potlatching each held one or more of a whole unbroken series of social positions which were ranked in order of greatness. These positions were distinguished from one another by particular names, by ceremonial prerogatives, like that of erecting a certain kind of potlatch pole, and by crests including house-paintings, masks and carved feasting dishes. All these distinctions were considered to have a history going back to the time when the ancestor of the position descended from heaven. All the positions were ranked not only in relation to the other positions but also according to the numaym or intratribal grouping to which they belonged and according to which of the thirteen Kwakiutl tribes the numayms belonged.[8] Both the great intricacy of the system and the confusion which resulted from the tragic decrease in the Kwakiutl population make it impossible to present it fully or in a way that would resolve all of the conflicts in the data but Table 14 and Figure 3 give a sample of the system of organiza-

[7] Boas, 1925, p. 343.

[8] The name Kwakiutl has been used for all the groups speaking the Kwakiutl dialect, including those speaking the Koskimo and the Newettee subdialects along with the Kwakiutl subdialect. The Koskimo can therefore add six tribes to the total. The number of tribes speaking the Kwakiutl subdialect can be counted as thirteen or twenty depending on whether the four subdivisions of the Kwakiutl proper and the five subdivisions of the Lekwiltoq are included in the total. Boas counts them as thirteen in the source given below. Ford gives the number of tribes as twenty-five (1941, p. 13) and (p. 11) also ranks the four septs of the Kwakiutl in places 1–4, whereas Boas ranks the Goasila and the Naqoaqtoq above the Kwakiutl, and assigns all four septs of the Kwakiutl to position 3(a–d).

tion. Table 14 lists thirteen Kwakiutl tribes in the order in which they received property at a potlatch given on the occasion of the death of a Mamaleleqala chief. The inflexible rule was that those greatest in rank received first at a potlatch. According to George Hunt, who gives this ranking of the Kwakiutl tribes, at this time there were 658 seats or positions in the various numayms of these tribes.[9] Figure 3 is abstracted from data given by Boas for one tribe, the Mamaleleqala, and is designed to show the unbroken hierarchy of the positions and of the numayms of this tribe which was fourth in rank of all Kwakiutl tribes.[10] Thus Figure 3 shows the top ranking potlatch position of this tribe to be the first position in the first numaym; while the lowest ranking position is the thirtieth seat in the fifth numaym. The total number of positions in this tribe comes to 131 and the lowest of all of these is considered to be above the highest position in the highest ranking numaym in the tribe next in rank to the Mamaleleqala.[11]

This "arbitrarily calibrated social structure," as Drucker has called it,[12] was the scheme for potlatching. At no place in the scheme was there an exact equivalence in ranking;[13] however, near equivalences were matched against each other for purposes of potlatching in a system so complex that the details are now beyond recovery. Even at the simplest level, the matching of the various tribes against one another, there seem to be inconsistencies,[14] perhaps arising out of such events as movements

[9] Boas, 1925, p. 91.

[10] The Mamaleleqala are fourth in greatness of rank according to the list given by Boas, 1897. pp. 28–332. The listing of the positions of the numayms of the Mamaleleqala is taken from the same source, pp. 339–340.

[11] Table 14 is taken from Boas, 1926, pp. 83–85. Since this is an eyewitness account reported by George Hunt who was a young man when he first began working for Jacobsen and Boas around the turn of the century, it probably happened around the years 1875–1885. Since the potlatch was given by the Mamaleleqala they must be included. They were fourth or fifth in the hierarchy. If they are inserted as fifth, all the numbers following must be increased by one. The linear hierarchy given by Ford (1941, p. 16) reverses positions 7 and 8, 10 and 11, 12 and 13. The first four listed are subdivisions of the Kwakiutl proper. Boas calls them septs. They are divisions superior to and including the numayms. Phonetics have been made to agree with those on Table 1.

[12] Drucker, 1939, p. 55.

[13] Drucker gives a most interesting Nootkan case of how the attempt to introduce an equivalence of ranking where the first chief of one tribe was equated with the first of a second tribe and so on was completely unsuccessful and unsatisfactory to all concerned (*Ibid.*, pp. 57–58).

[14] Boas gives the following matching in 1897, p. 343:

Guē'tEla vs. Ma'malēleqala; Q!ō' moyuē vs. Qoēxsōt'ēnôx;
Q!ō'mk·ūtîs vs. NE'mqîc; Wā'las Kwakiutl vs. Lau'itsîs.

In the same source, pp. 328–332, the rank order of the tribes given indicates that Q!ō'mk·ūtîs should be matched with Lau'itsîs and Wā'las Kwakiutl with NE'mqîc.

of tribes and numayms in the area, or perhaps the results of potlatch contests in which tables were turned and less exalted positions, or groupings of them came to have higher rank.[15] Since it was a convention to claim always that the positions and their ranking went back to the time of "the myth people" the record of the re-rankings resulting from such upsets is lost, even though we know them to have occurred, for there are many stories of great victories and ignominious defeats, and

TABLE 14

Potlatch Ranking of Thirteen Kwakiutl Tribes

Guē'tEla	1
Q'ō'moyuē	2
Wa'las Kwakiutl	3
Q'ō'mk·ūtis	4
NE'mqic	5
Lau'itsis	6
Mātilpē	7
T'Ena'xtax	8
A'wa-iLala	9
Qoē'xsōt'ēnôx	10
Ts'ā'watEēnôx	11
Haxuā'mîs	12
Guau'aēnôx	13

each potlatch is dramatized as the wholehearted attempt to live up to a position and maintain its greatness against a rival making an equally intense effort to challenge it.

The system, especially in connection with potlatch finances, was so complex that Charles Nowell, the Kwakiutl chief, could say after more than half a lifetime of experience and concern with its details, "I still don't know everything about it."[16] Aside from possessing a complexity which seems to have been a source of intellectual interest, at least to

[15] Boas, 1897, p. 332.
[16] Ford, 1941, p. 106.

Figure 4
Kwakiutl Social Organization
As A Series of Ranked Positions

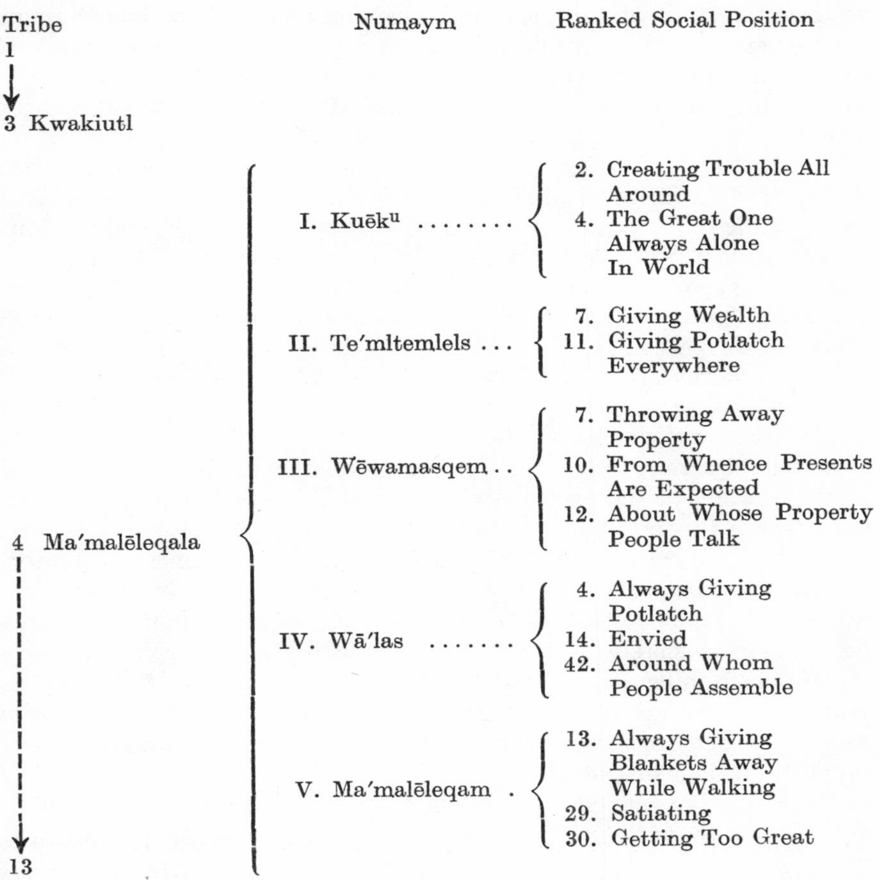

Ranked positions are not available for all tribes but Figure 3 (after Boas, 1897, pp. 339–340) gives one hundred and thirty-one individual ranked positions for the five numayms of the Ma'malēleqala tribe. Only a sampling is given here in order to clarify the system and to indicate the type of name used of the potlatch positions. Tribal names (1–13) appear in Table 1 of this paper.

some Kwakiutl,[17] two further characteristics of this social system need to be brought out. The first is that the drastic population decline which followed on contact and extended well into the historical period could not and did not attack the principles on which the system rested. There was confusion in the consistency of the record; there was a greater number of positions in proportion to the population; and it is quite possible that individuals from hereditary lines which had been those of commoners before, without claim to any potlatch position, somehow gained one of the lower positions, although we know of one case where the attempt to do so was unsuccessful.[18] Nevertheless, the idea of a whole series of individually held social ranks remained.

The final and most significant point about this social structure is that it is here of all the areas of Kwakiutl life that a genuine scarcity exists. The ranking of the positions according to greatness and the elaborations of each of them by their association with particular names, origin myths, crests and prerogatives, emphasize their relative scarcity value at every point. As Mead has put it: "The Kwakiutl in the midst of plenty build their . . . fierce competition on an artificially constructed scarcity of titles and prerogatives."[19] In what might be called their "economic life" the Kwakiutl are virtuoso technicians and extravagant producers and storers. It is in their "social life" that they "economize."

A basic dynamic of the Kwakiutl potlatch, therefore, is to be found in the relation of the arbitrarily determined scarcity of potlatch positions to the superabundance of some economic goods. It was, however, the addition of certain financial concepts: credit, investment and interest, that maximized the potlatch. By these means far more impressive quantities of goods could be distributed at a potlatch than could have been acquired merely by a parsimonious hoarding of surpluses; and a far greater number of individuals of all tribes and numayms were involved in a network of debtor-creditor relations than merely those who were "matched" against each other alternately to receive and distribute property in their potlatches.

The property received by a man in a potlatch was no free and wanton gift. He was not at liberty to refuse it, even though accepting it obligated

[17] The Kwakiutl held the idea that the oldest children in a family were foolish while the youngest were clever, an idea which is also to be found in European fairy and folk tales. It was, therefore, to the younger sons that the offices of counter and tally keeper were usually given. Both these offices required expert knowledge of all the Kwakiutl positions and their ranks (Boas, 1925, p. 59).

[18] This was the case of the man who was able to buy an expensive copper with the earnings made by his wife and three daughters as prostitutes in Victoria. The death of all the women and his own illness convinced him that sorcery was being directed against them for such presumption and he gave up the copper to a proper chief and position holder (*Ibid.*, pp. 94–95).

[19] Mead, 1937, p. 466.

him to make a return at another potlatch not only of the original amount but of twice as much, if this return was made, as was usual, in a period of about a year. This gave potlatching its forced loan and investment aspects, since a man was alternately debtor and creditor for amounts that were increasing at a geometric rate.

In a report about potlatching first published in the Victoria *Province* and calculated to diminish the intolerance of the Canadians of the area by making the practice more understandable to them, Boas even compares it to life insurance.[20] There is an analogy. Because potlatching was the office of an inherited position and one which from their point of view had existed from the beginning of history and was eternal, the death of an incumbent did not wipe out potlatch property due his heir and the next holder of the position.[21] The analogy breaks down somewhat when it is recognized that the heir to the position also had to take over any obligations to creditors. Perhaps comparing it to life insurance involves this inaccuracy but there is in another sense considerable truth in the analogy. Whether the heir came into debts or credits, he did come fully into the system in which all honor existed. The same Canadians who condemned the potlatch, undoubtedly held the idea that the future of heirs should be underwritten with money enough for at least the necessities of life. Under circumstances where these necessities were guaranteed equally to all and where differences in wealth did not mean invidious distinctions in consumption patterns or planes of living, they, like the Kwakiutl, might have tried to assure less material conditions of honor and respectability.

It might well be claimed that the potlatch also had the character of an investment. The cycles of giving and receiving, of forcing and obligation to make a return greater than the original gift or being placed under such an obligation, were associated with other financial developments in a way which makes the use of such terminology appropriate. First, there is a well worked out system of interest rates on loans, constructed on the principle that the return payment must increase with the term of the loan. Table 15 reproduces these "interest rates" which are excessive from our point of view. As a detailed description of the loans and borrowings preceding a potlatch will show, the Kwakiutl principle

[20] Boas, Victoria *Province*, Feb. 11, 1897, quoted in Keithahn, 1945, pp. 104—105. A verbatim repetition of this article may be found in Boas, 1898, pp. 54—55.

[21] Succession to a potlatch position was usually decided before the holder of the position died. In effect, he retired from the position in order to give it to the heir when the heir was considered old enough to handle its responsibilities. The rule of primogeniture obtained and if the first-born was a girl, she was given a man's name in her succession to the potlatch position. The rule of primogeniture can be documented in the primary data (Boas, 1925, p. 91).

is entirely consistent with their expectation that repayment was certain, because the entire social status of the borrower was at stake, and that the more time a man had the more he could amass through his loans and potlatches.[22] A man who received property at a potlatch was expected to make the return at another potlatch in about a year. Thus the 100

TABLE 15[23]

Kwakiutl Interest Rates
For Different Lengths of Time

Term	Number of Blankets Borrowed	Lek!o or the return Demanded	Interest Rate
Under 6 months	5	6	20 %
6 months	5	7	40 %
12 months	5	10	100 %
12 months under circumstances where the borrower has poor credit	5	17	233 %

per cent interest figure as in Table 15 is found to be characteristic of most potlatches. Preparatory to every potlatch there was, however, a complicated series of small loans at smaller interest rates, since a shorter term was involved. This produced the vast network of debtor-creditor

[22] Again it is necessary to note that our financial operations are connected with our subsistence, with the planes of living of not only individuals but also of whole populations. Our pattern of financial operations is therefore consistent with the fact that investment in enterprises which are firmly grounded in the customary and continuous living habits of the people bring a certain but small return under conditions of competition, while investment in new enterprises will, if successful, be making new connections with the great market created by living habits and will have greater rewards for a time due to lack of competition and the relative scarcity of the new economic good.

[23] Boas, 1897, p. 341. It is claimed that the interest varies around 25 per cent depending on the kindness of the creditor.

For a very short time no interest is required.

In order for a borrower with poor credit to receive a loan even at these interest rates he must pawn his name for a year. This means, of course, that he is out of the potlatch system for this period. The figures given in the source are a return of 100 blankets for a loan of thirty. Using the base of five it will be seen that a return of seventeen is slightly greater than 233%.

relations that has been mentioned as creating ties between men of all the numayms and tribes and as being the means of amassing the very impressive amounts distributed in the potlatch itself. Because it was the potlatch that was absorbing and dramatic in the highest degree, far more complete details exist about it than about the preparatory loans. An additional difficulty is that the preparations and the potlatches formed together such a continuous process that for the most part no obvious starting point for description and analysis can be found.

There is, however, one account which facilitates an understanding of the process. This concerns the borrowings of a boy in preparation for his first potlatch at which he will receive his third or man's name and succeed to his father's potlatch position. Figure 5 describes this in detail. Here the boy begins by borrowing from the members of his own tribe at the customary interest rates. He lends this capital, probably to those of his own numaym as well as his own tribe, as specified in the text, because the return made to him is within a very brief period and, contrary to the usual schedule of interest rates, is treble the amount loaned. There seem, in other words, to be special measures taken here to help him get started in potlatching. He must repay them 100 per cent interest for the extra 100 blankets which he has received over and above the expected return of the 100 blankets he loaned them, plus 100 per cent interest or 200 blankets. With his greatly increased capital of 300 blankets, he is now able to make loans to his friends which at the end of ten months bring him back his capital plus 50% interest.[24] The text does not make it clear at this point whether the potlatch includes the public repayment of these debts to the members of his own tribe. In any case, this repayment is described as the first part of the ceremony at which he enters the potlatch system and immediately following it he takes his potlatch name and his father's potlatch position and distributes property to men outside his own numaym, and tribe, thus beginning a potlatch relationship with them which will continue until he passes his position on to his successor. The question as to whether the repayment of his debts is technically part of the potlatch is insignificant beside the fact that he has been able to amass, in his financial operations, property in quantities sufficient to make the proper showing for a potlatch.

[24] Boas, 1897, pp. 341–342. Boas says that at this point he may have 400 blankets. I have assigned him fifty more, because 400 blankets would be just enough to permit him to repay his debts at the year's end and yet, the text makes it clear that he not only makes this repayment but also sells enough blankets to buy food for a feast and to distribute blankets to members of the other tribes and clans, as Boas puts it, with whom he has not been previously connected in loans or potlatching. It is possible, of course, that his father has provided him with these extra blankets. Since Boas' account is a generalized one, rather than a description of events as they actually occurred in a particular case, it does not misrepresent the system to add these fifty blankets to the total.

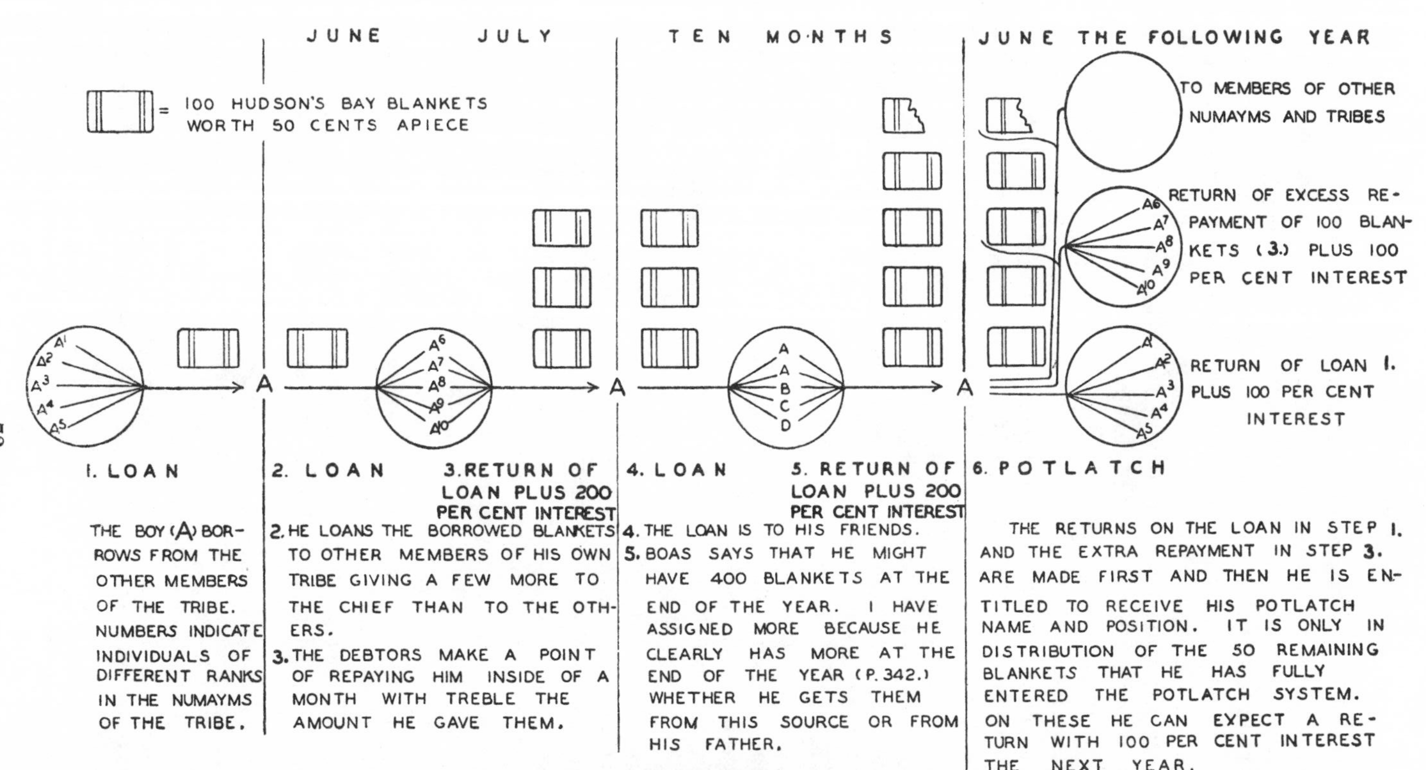

Fig. 5. Loans and Returns in Preparation for a Kwakiutl Potlatch (after Boas, 1897, pp. 341–342).

An actual case detailing the financial preparations for several closely related potlatches can be found in the biography of Charles Nowell.[25] These potlatches revolve around the purchase of a copper[26] for Charles Nowell by his father-in-law, Lagius. The making of loans which would fall due at the end of the year was the first step following the decision of Lagius, Charles Nowell, and his brother, Owadi, to collaborate in this affair and following the decision of the Tlowitsis chief to sell his copper, named "to clean everything out of the house," to them:

> When Lagius took hold of the copper, he says: "I have now received your copper, which you want to sell, and I'll only keep it one day, (that means one year) and then I'll buy it from you. I will give you a thousand dollars as a pillow till I pay the rest. I have been looking for a copper as big as this, for I have been awake every night, wanting to get a copper for my daughter's husband."
>
> Then he counted out the thousand dollars, which the Tlowitsis chief took and said to all the people: "This money is ready to be loaned out. All the time Lagius will pay for my copper I will collect this money, which is to be paid 100 percent back to me, and then it will be paid to Lagius." Lagius also stood up and say he had some money to loan out. My brother also says he has money to loan out.
>
> When Lagius or I or my brother loan out blankets, before we pay for the copper, we loan to anybody that wants them. Maybe they want to buy some food. Maybe they owe somebody else some money, and the owner of that money wants to collect from him; if he is unable to pay himself, he asks for the amount he is shy, to pay. Or maybe he wants to sleep with a girl and wants to get money for that. So he goes to one of us and asks us for the money. He then uses it for whatever he wants. Then comes the time when we call in our money, because we are going to buy the copper. So we go to him and asks him to pay, and we collect what we had loaned.[27]

There is not full enough information in the text about the sources of all the funds involved, but partly as a result of these loans, 14,500 blankets were finally available for the purchase of the copper! These went to the Tlowitsis chief for the copper and he gave a great potlatch with them. The copper and $500 went to Charles Nowell, who gave a potlatch "to the Fort Ruperts" with the $500 and then handed over

[25] Ford, 1941, pp. 168–185. The details of this case follow very closely the general description of the purchase of a copper to be found in Boas, 1897, pp. 344–345.

[26] Coppers will be described below.

[27] Ford, 1941, pp. 169–170. The statement that people might borrow in order to buy food seems to contradict the claims that have been made that Kwakiutl subsistence activities continued and that the potlatch was far removed from subsistence activities. The date of this purchase of a copper is given as 1901. At this time the Kwakiutl were certainly earning their own living directly. Perhaps they might want to have money with which to buy store foods for the feasts which always accompanied potlatches. In this case store foods would be in the same class as silk scarves or zinc washboilers. They would not be any vital part of "their living."

the copper to his brother to sell, "so he could give a potlatch."[28] Although the brother sold the copper for more than had been paid for it, he died before he had received the full purchase price and before he had collected the loans due him. Under the pretext of having to obey the Canadian law against potlatching,[29] some of the debtors defaulted and Charles Nowell was not fully repaid for the copper he had given his brother. Nevertheless this same copper was sold again, and, as in all the previous sales, probably brought an amount far in excess of its preceding valuation.

These two examples demonstrate the importance of the part played by interest in the potlatch cycle. The amount of property distributed at the potlatch itself or at the peak of the cycle increased yearly at a geometric ratio because of the 100 per cent interest rate. Since men were matched against each other and alternately gave and received, one of them was responsible for distributing four times the amount of property he had distributed the time before and one of them was receiving four times what he had received two years earlier. The scheme would be as follows:

1st year ..... A gives x blankets to B
2nd year ..... B gives 2 x blankets to A
3rd year ..... A gives 4 x blankets to B
4th year ..... B gives 8 x blankets to A.

Without the vast network of small loans made in the intervening period at proportional rates of interest such yearly and biennial increases would be inconceivable.

At this point two interesting and pertinent questions about the Kwakiutl potlatch system arise: first, were there ever enough actual blankets and other potlatch goods to cover all the outstanding obligations and, second, how could a system associated with these extravagant interest rates, avoid a collapse?

The workings of the Kwakiutl potlatch were based upon credit. There never existed sufficient potlatch goods, especially blankets, to cover all the transactions in them. Boas states that an attempt of all the creditors to call in their loans would result in a "disastrous panic."[30] There is one

[28] *Ibid.*, p. 178. These were the people of his own tribe.

[29] As will be seen in the historical material which follows, the Indian Act forbidding potlatches and winter dances had very little restraining effect on potlatching at any rate. Charles Nowell was potlatching twenty years after the incident given above (p. 224) and the jail term he served in 1921 for potlatching did not prevent him from giving potlatches after this (see pp. 226–228). Men with relatively large debts, and perhaps, a relatively inferior status in the potlatch social system, might be expected to be among the first to become "law-abiding."

[30] Boas, 1898, pp. 54–55.

measure of the degree to which this was a credit system: it was claimed by Boas that in a village of 150 people, where only 400 blankets existed, debts were owed to the amount of 75,000 blankets![31] Very large numbers of real blankets were actually collected, displayed and distributed at potlatches.[32] Yet, even then, the time of all times to make magnificent displays, there seem often not to have been the number of blankets in terms of which the total glory of the potlatch was summarized. Sometimes the value of a canoe would be expressed as, say, 400 blankets, or $1,000 Canadian money as 2,000 blankets.[33] Sometimes it would happen that a man would receive merely a tally stick worth a certain number of blankets, because he had, for his own purposes, collected in advance the blankets he would otherwise have received in the potlatch.

A credit system in which the prevailing interest rates would result in the doubling of the debt or credit each succeeding year and in which no participant could refuse the debt obligations given to him would seem due to collapse in a few years. Had ten blankets been "given" in the original potlatch, 4,320 would be required for the potlatch ten years later. Potlatches, like those mentioned in the literature, involving hundreds or thousands of blankets would in a few years call forth other potlatches involving astronomical figures.

The reason a collapse did not occur and that potlatching as a financial system remained meaningful and tied to reality was that the system had as well developed means for the destruction of credit as it had for its phenomenal growth. In this the "coppers" had the outstanding part.[34] These beaten sheets of copper were slightly convex and approximately two to two and one-half feet in length. The top half was flaring, somewhat wider than the bottom, and bore an engraving in black lead which represented the face of the crest animal of the first owner. A raised T-shaped ridge divided the bottom part in half and separated it from the engraved part. The value of a copper depended entirely upon the amount of property that had been paid for it and then given away in the potlatch in which it had last changed hands. Boas has compared the function of these coppers to that of bank notes of high denomination. Coppers were often individualized by a name which boasted of the number of blankets they would bring in their purchase, "all other coppers are ashamed to look at it," "making the house empty of blankets," "looking below" (in order to find blankets with which to buy it).[35]

These coppers were the currency of rivalry in the everlasting contest between the two position holders the hierarchical system had matched

[31] Boas, class notes, Barnard College, 1921.
[32] The photographs in Boas, 1897, are very informative on this point.
[33] Ford, 1941, p. 172.
[34] See frontispiece for illustration.
[35] Boas, 1897, pp. 342, 344, 354.

and opposed to one another. The buying, selling and, finally, the destruction of a copper was done only between rivals. Because this potlatching with coppers was considered a matter of such consequence and because the shameful defeat of a man in this greatest of contests reflected upon all those of his numaym and tribe, he was ordinarily helped by them in the purchase of a copper from his rival, just as he distributed to them the property he received from his rival through the sale of the copper. As long as the two rivals could keep up with one another with the help of their respective groups, whatever they did, the buying or selling of coppers, or even the partial destruction of them,[36] was profitable to both and at a rate we should regard as fantastic.

It is only in the total destruction of a copper that a profitless act can be found. Then, credits were destroyed. Then, the continuous series of cycles where each succeeding peak was twice the height of the one before was finally broken. This was the surpassing feat, and if the rival could not match it and destroy a copper of equal or greater value, by throwing it into the fire or the sea, he was beaten and disgraced even though he might still be wealthier in property and credits than his rival who had spent all his resources for the victory. Such destruction was above all else the theme of the grandiloquent songs which were sung at potlatches as one of the privileges associated with a potlatch position. An example is the song of Ēwanuẋ[x] Dzē, Chief of the Maămtag·ila:

> Let our property remain alive (under the attacks) of the reckless chief!
> Let our copper remain unbroken by the reckless chief. Ye, yaa ha.
> Do not let our chief do so! He himself made disappear those who owned the names of (our) property, of the great copper made expensive by him, the great surpassing one, the great copper cutter, the great one who throws (coppers) into the sea. This reckless chief. Ye, yaa ha!
> ....[37]

There are many accounts in the literature of men who rise to these heights in potlatching with coppers.[38] It is made very clear that this is the flagrant case in the Kwakiutl potlatch system, that the "reckless," meaning "profitless," destruction of coppers represents the pinnacle of

[36] There was a fixed order in which parts of a copper were to be broken off: upper right, lower left, upper left, and lower right. Counting the remaining T-shaped ridge, this yielded five parts. If a man breaks a copper into these pieces and gives them to his rival, and, if the rival is able to do the same thing with a copper of equal or greater value and to make a return of both coppers, the value of both coppers is enhanced. Usually one piece is broken off at a time and the pieces of a copper then become scattered widely in the region. Under these circumstances, if all the pieces are bought up and welded together, the total value of the copper is greatly increased (*Ibid.*, p. 354).

[37] Boas, 1921, Part II, p. 1285. Quoted in part.

[38] Boas, 1897, pp. 354–357, 556, 564, 621–622; 1910, pp. 83–95; 1921, Part II, pp. 861–862, 1115–1117, 1285–1288; 1925, pp. 13, 15, 79, 85–87, 171, 185, 189, 193–195, 215–229, 283–298; Dawson, 1887, pp. 19ff; Ford, 1941, pp. 20–22, 26–27, 101, 180–182; and Hunt, 1906, pp. 108–136.

ambition. An account in the biography of Charles Nowell illustrates how desperate a contest this was in spite of the fact that victorious potlatching meant neither command over the means of production from which all gained their living nor power over people, except in the sense that the rival was crushed by shame.

To give the background of the account: Two Mamaleleqala chiefs "drown" or throw into the sea, the T-shaped ridges of two coppers they possess. This is to squelch the opposition to their nephew whom they wish to set up in a potlatch position. One of these pieces of copper is meant for Whanuk and one for Charley Wilson, both of whom oppose the nephew. Then a Tlowitsis chief, Tlatli-litla, buys a very expensive copper, breaks off the upper right and lower left parts and gives them to the Mamaleleqala chiefs. The rest of the story is in the words of Charles Nowell:

> This was a wonderful thing that he did. When we came to Alert Bay about six months after that and all the people were here to a potlatch, one of those Mamaleleqala chiefs died. He wasn't sick at all – he just dropped down. The other one went to Fraser River that summer, and he also died there without being sick – just dropped down dead. They worried too much how they are going to get a copper big enough to break for this chief that has broken a copper for them, and that is why they died. They tried ever since Tlatli-litla break this copper for them to get a copper from the owners of other coppers, but they were too old to be trusted with a copper, and were thought unable to buy any more coppers.
>
> About eight or ten years after this, Whanuk got a copper, and at his potlatch he told the young men here at Alert Bay to take this copper out in front of the village and drown it – all of it, the whole thing. This was long after the men that had drowned him with his copper had died, but he didn't want to be spoken of as drowned by this copper. About seven years ago Charley Wilson gave a grease potlatch to all the tribes and he also got a copper and cut a piece of it and throwed it in the water to drown it, but he didn't mention the name of the man who drowned him. He should have put the whole thing in the water the same as Whanuk did. I don't see what he wants to keep it for.[39]

Thus, potlatching can include the destruction as well as the distribution of property. One factor which has been omitted from the description of potlatching so far is that all potlatching included feasting as part of its ceremonial and public quality. The guest at a potlatch received food as well as blankets. Here too, most potlatches seem to have been relatively sober affairs, where the chief did not "rise too high" and perform "reckless" acts. Yet the greatest of all were feasts in which actual destruction occurred. The most famous of these were the grease

[39] Ford, 1941, pp. 180–182. It is unfortunate that Ford has chosen to reproduce Charley Nowell's somewhat broken English. This occasionally gives the impression that he is not well informed or intelligent. The reader must remember that Charles Nowell is "literate" in every phase of his own culture and that his native language and the one he customarily speaks is Kwakiutl.

feasts in which box after box of oulachen oil was poured upon the fire causing it to burn so furiously that it singed the blankets worn by the guests or made the roof boards catch fire.[40] Such deeds brought extra glory.

The main preoccupation of the Kwakiutl potlatcher, however, was with high finance as a method of rivalry. This conclusion can be found consistently in all the writings of students of the Kwakiutl potlatch, although it is at times somewhat obscured by differences in approach and emphasis on points of special interest. The massive work of Boas on Kwakiutl has, of course, formed the basis of all subsequent work, but this would not predetermine the kind of conclusion drawn, as any previous conclusions can be disregarded and a reinterpretation made on the basis of the facts alone.[41] Thus Adam,[42] Barnett,[43] Benedict,[44] Boas,[45] Bunzel,[46] Dawson,[47] Ford,[48] Goldman and Mead[49] are in substantial agreement.

The majority of these writers also point out the curious but wholly reasonable fact that in order for there to be dramatic emphasis on rivalry and competition in the Kwakiutl potlatch and in Kwakiutl life there had also to be a very great amount of cooperation.[50] Boas, for example, notes that:

> The leading motive of their lives is the limitless pursuit of gaining social prestige and of holding on to what has been gained, and the intense feeling of inferiority and shame if even the slightest part of prestige has been lost.

[40] Boas, 1921, pp. 774–775: "...At the same time the four young men who handle the ladles dip them into the oil; and when they are full, they pour the oil into the fire; and then those who try to put out the fire run away on account of the heat, for the oil and the blankets are burning together; and then the host takes the oil and pours it among his rivals.

"Nolis, who died some time ago at Alert Bay, tried to put out the fire with seven canoes, and he had the oil poured on his face by the great host of the Lawet!ses. Besides, he put on four hundred blankets. The house was nearly burned. All the roof boards were burned. And this is the most real attempt at putting out the fire of a feast that I have seen. The feast giver of the Lawets!es had two hundred blankets and five canoes, and also small coppers. This is the worst thing that chiefs do when they really get angry, and at such times the house-dishes (heirloom crests) are scorched by the fire."

[41] This has certainly been the case with many ethnographies, e. g., that of the Ba-Thonga by the missionary, Junod.

[42] Adam, 1922, pp. 27–45.

[43] Barnett, 1938, pp. 349–358.

[44] Benedict, 1934, pp. 173–222.

[45] Boas, see bibliography.

[46] Bunzel, 1938, pp. 357–361.

[47] Dawson, 1887, pp. 19ff. This brief account is independent of any of Boas' work.

[48] Ford, 1941.

[49] Goldman, 1937, pp. 180–209, 459–501.

[50] The writings of Benedict and Dawson form an exception.

> This is manifest not only in the attempts to gain a coveted high position, but equally in the endeavor to be considered the most atrocious member of the tribe. . . .
>
> These tendencies are so striking that the amiable qualities that appear in intimate family life are easily overlooked. These are not by any means absent . . .[51]

Mead notes in her interpretation of all the societies studied in connection with the problem of cooperation and competition:

> In a study devoted to cooperation and competition, there was no doubt that the Kwakiutl were grossly competitive, . . .
>
> Nevertheless, no society is exclusively competitive or exclusively cooperative. The very existence of highly competitive groups implies cooperation within the groups. Both competitive and cooperative habits must exist within the society. There is furious competition among the Kwakiutl at one stratum of the society – among the ranking chiefs – but within the household of each chief cooperation is mandatory for the amassing of the wealth that is distributed or destroyed.[52]

In discussing the potlatch as an event, Barnett draws attention to certain cooperative features it possessed:

> Such contests are therefore latent in any potlatch, but as a patterned response their elaboration is abnormal from an areal standpoint. . . .
>
> Indeed, in the descriptions of the famous Kwakiutl contests attention is so completely centered upon the antagonistic attitudes of the two rivals that an important fact is lost sight of; namely that they are only the principals in a drama, which like all dramas, is for the benefit of spectators.[53]

There are many other examples of the cooperative qualities in Kwakiutl family life, in the individual Kwakiutl numaym and tribe in its rivalry with others, and even in the rivalry of the potlatch situation itself.[54] Members of a young man's own group helped him with the giving of his first potlatch and the purchase of his first copper. The buying and selling of coppers always involved the numayms and tribes of which the rivals were members. The grandeur of the 14,500 blanket potlatch previously described was a product of the joint efforts of Charles Nowell, his brother and his father-in-law.

It is amusing, however, to see in all the wealth of data that exists on the Kwakiutl potlatch how underplayed, and even how secretive and underhanded, these cooperative elements are. A statement of Charles Nowell demonstrates this most effectively:

> Any time I feel like giving a feast or a potlatch after I was married, I get my own money and give it to Lagius, and he give it back to me to give a feast or a potlatch. This is for the honor of my child and most times he would add some of his own money to it to make it more. And when I give the feast or potlatch, I say the money comes from him, after my child was

[51] Boas, 1938, p. 685.

[52] Mead, 1937, pp. 459–460.

[53] Barnett, 1938, pp. 356–357.

[54] Boas, 1897, pp. 341–342, 344–352, 353–354; and 1921, Pt. 2, pp. 1333–1344.

born I did this, and every time a child of mine comes to the time when the baby begins to eat, I do this. Any time the child begins to play and gets hurt, I give money to Lagius and he gives it back to me, and I give it away to wipe the blood of the child's wounds. A good son-in-law would do this to his wife's father. I always did it for my wife's father's good name and my child's good name, and the way I do it nobody knows it except Lagius and myself, and everybody thinks it is all his money I am spending, except the others know that is what they should do themselves and that I probably do it that way.[55]

To summarize the general characteristics of the Kwakiutl potlatch: its "objective" features are an economy many stages removed from ordinary subsistence activities, an elaborate hierarchy of social positions possessing scarcity value, and the development of so complex a scheme of credit, investment and interest that it is accurately descriptive to term it "finance." All these objective features are manipulated to accord to the demands of a psychology based on rivalry to such an extent that the real cooperation which sustained it was a furtive affair.

[55] Ford, 1941, p. 156.

CHAPTER FOUR

History of the Kwakiutl Potlatch

Continuity of the Potlatch in the Historical Record

The continuity of the Kwakiutl potlatch throughout the historical period can be established beyond doubt. There are reports of Kwakiutl potlatching for twenty-eight of the fifty-two years between 1872 and 1924. In some cases, there are more than one in a year. The total record can be extended backward to 1866 when the traveller John Keast Lord saw a copper at Fort Rupert for which fifteen slaves and 200 blankets had been paid;[1] and forward to include a potlatch given by Charles Nowell's son-in-law[2] at a date which can be set with reasonable certainty as 1936.[3]

The majority of these reports on Kwakiutl potlatching come from the various Indian agents and are censorious. It is especially important to recognize that the Kwakiutl continued their potlatching in spite of the heavy disapproval of all the Europeans in the area agents, missionaries, everyone, with the one or two ethnologists being the only discoverable exceptions; and also in spite of whatever pressures these groups were able to exert including specific legal restrictions.

The agency reports were either hopeful that potlatching had been dissipating its final strength and was soon to disappear, a note that was struck as early as 1872, or they showed exasperation and discouragment because the potlatch remained a huge and immovable block to "progress" and the "attainment of civilization." Selections from these reports and statements of eye-witness accounts of potlatches of known date are reproduced below.

1872 — The chiefs still however employ practices peculiar to themselves, in order to maintain as large a share of influence as possible with their people. Some of them donate, under the name of "Potlatches", to their people, blankets, food, firearms, etc., etc. The gifts are dealt out with profusion, but it is attended with a strange feature; for an equivalent in return at a future gathering is expected to be presented. The Superintendent considers that these usages have an injurious tendency and encourage idleness, and expresses a hope the custom will in time become obsolete.[4]

1881 — (Adrian Jacobsen witnessed the winter dances and associated potlatches of the Kwakiutl). . . . .

[1] Lord, 1866, Vol. 1, p. 257.

[2] Ford, 1941, pp. 225–226.

[3] There has been no attempt to get information on the Kwakiutl for the last decade.

[4] Canada. Annual Report on Indian Affairs, 1872, p. 10.

Naturally at this tribal gathering one chief tried to outdo another and maintained his prestige by dividing up and distributing the property he had collected. In this way hundreds, even thousands, of blankets passed from hand to hand each day; at the same time contests were arranged, quarrels settled, betrothals made and so forth. The soul of the whole affair was the Kwakiutl chief who lived in Ft. Rupert.[5]

1881 — Surrounded with boxes of property all ready for the "potlatch" on which their whole souls are fixed now more than ever, they turn a deaf ear to any suggestion to purchase a little rice, tea or sugar for their suffering progeny. . . . Out of this apathetic state the Agent must endeavor to lift them ere any hopes of bettering them can be expected. . . .

I may safely say that one and all, so far, have met me cordially and expressed their entire concurrence in the system now being inaugurated by the Government for bettering their condition.

Of course, I have to expect, for the present, the doubts of many as regards the wisdom of doing away with the "Potlatch". This custom has of late years, increased to a very great extent; and those most interested who are principally the old chiefs, have offered a most determined opposition.

Many others, however, would be glad to see it abolished; and I look for assistance to these in putting it down when the proper time comes. In fairness to those who have so much at stake, and in order to allow them to collect their debts, I have stated that a year or two hence it must be discontinued.[6]

1882 — The question of "potlatching" has engaged my most serious attention.

A general tone of despondency prevails among the elders of the different tribes on account of their being obliged to give up this old custom.

I have pointed out to them over and over again, the evils attending it, which the younger members do not fail to recognize, and even appreciate its intended abolishment.

They had had due warning, and those who in future choose to risk or lend their property will experience a difficulty in recovering it.[7]

1883 — The energy they display in collecting property is certainly remarkable . . . but unfortunately, so much is squandered at feasts and otherwise, that they have not as they ought to have, continuous comfort, or continuous wholesome food.[8]

1885 — In regard the act of relating to the prohibition of the celebration of their two most heathenish customs, (i. e. the potlatch and the winter dance) each tribe has been furnished with the fullest information, and of the penalty attached to its infringement. The tribes are now assembled at three separate localities, and they have been notified that, on their dispersion, no future gatherings will be allowed, without incurring the full penalty of the law.

It is, however, evident from their deportment and conversation, that they are watching the course of events in the south, still hoping that the law will not be carried into effect.[9]

1887 — The Indians belonging to the Kwaw-kewlth Band who live at Fort Rupert, moved away in a body last October, to pay a visit to the Nim-keesh Indians at Alert Bay, and have been with them and the band at Mah-ma-lil-le-kullah ever since. (Note: potlatches were invariably the reason for such gatherings) . . .

[5] Jacobsen, 1884, pp. 121–122. Translated by the writer.

[6] Canada. Annual Report on Indian Affairs, Blenkinsop, 1881, pp. 170–171.

[7] *Ibid.*, Blenkinsop, 1882, p. 66.

[8] *Ibid.*, Blenkinsop, 1883, p. 48.

[9] *Ibid.*, 1885, p. 84.

They are no doubt anxiously looking to see whether any steps have been taken in other parts towards the suppression of the "Potlatch", which custom they cling to with pertinacity, and which, I am convinced, is at the root of all the vices amongst these Indians, and the gatherings to intimidate the younger ones who show any desire for reformation, and I doubt whether any-one has any idea of the persecutions these younger members have to undergo.[10]

1888 — In regard to the Potlatch there are tokens that it must soon undergo a marked change, or gradually die out. The reason for this is that of late years blankets have so depreciated in value that few if any new blankets are bought as the purchase entails a loss. New blankets cannot be purchased for less than $2.50 a pair, and they are only worth $1.50 among themselves, consequently they are becoming very scarce, and money is gradually taking their place. While visiting the Mar-ma-lil-li-kulla tribe recently it was forcibly impressed upon me, as small pieces of stick were often given in lieu of blankets, to be redeemed as soon as the man was able. I also saw a good deal of silver given away, perhaps as much as three or four hundred dollars, at a Potlatch that took place while I was there.[11]

1889 — About twelve hundred of the eighteen hundred odd Indians in this agency congregated within twenty miles of Alert Bay . . ., and I spent a fort-night among them in March. They were quite orderly and well behaved while I was there. Some of their superstitious practices are no doubt objectionable, but these they seem inclined to give up readily enough; only to the Potlatch do they cling with great pertinacity. I notified them that after this I should put the law in force in regard to the Potlatch and during the summer I had a man arrested and sent to Victoria, but owing to some informality in the committment he was discharged, which will necessitate another man being sent down and imprisoned before the Indians will believe that the law must be obeyed.[12]

1890 — I am sorry to say that I cannot report any improvement among these Indians; they seem to have given themselves up again to the "Potlatch", which has absorbed the whole of their time and energies during the last ten months, and, in consequence they have earned very little money, though they could all have obtained remunerative employment at the different canneries had they chosen to work. I think, however, that there is a desire for improvement among numbers of the young men and women, but circum-stances have combined to encourage the older people in their attempts to prevent any progress being made.[13]

1893 — The Ma-ma-lil-li-kulla Indians have availed themselves rather tardily of the Government grant given to them to rebuild their houses destroyed by fire, they being under the impression that, if they accepted the grant, they would not be allowed to build any more large houses, and consequently would not be able any longer to hold their potlatch and dances.[14]

Winter of 1894–1895 — At Fort Rupert Boas witnessed a potlatch at which a copper was sold for 4,200 blankets.[15]

Fall of 1895 — Boas witnessed a series of potlatches at Fort Rupert: (1) Nov. 22, a potlatch of 120 blankets, 2,000 silver bracelets, 40 button blankets; (2) Nov. 23, a potlatch of 6 button blankets, 40 blankets and calico for the women

[10] *Ibid.*, 1887, pp. 109–110.
[11] *Ibid.*, Pidcock, 1888, p. 104.
[12] *Ibid.*, 1889, p. 102.
[13] *Ibid.*, 1890, p. 75.
[14] *Ibid.*, 1893, p. 124.
[15] Boas, 1897, pp. 346–353.

and children; and (3) Nov. 23, a Koskimo "gives" a copper worth 500 blankets to a Kwakiutl.[16]

1900 — As long as they still continue the custom of distributing property they will not accumulate money for any better purpose, but this custom is gradually dying out among the younger members who no longer take the same interest in it that they used to do.[17]

1904 — The Indians of this agency have been quite peaceable and quiet during the past year, except on one occasion, when an attempt was made to break up their potlatch at Fort Rupert; otherwise they have been doing very well. As long as the different bands are kept separate and confined to their reserves, there is no trouble; but when they all congregate in one village, as they are in the habit of doing in the winter months, they are rather difficult to manage. . . . . .

These Indians have been, and are yet, for that matter, most antagonistic to the white race.[18]

1905 — The Indians have been very quiet and peaceable during the past year. I had only one inconsiderable trouble this year, and that was in breaking up their potlatch at Mamalillikulla last April; they seemed to have got the idea that I was interfering with their ceremonies in opposition to the department.[19]

1906 — January, 1906, a number of girls were sold at prices ranging from three hundred to twelve hundred dollars. The latter figure was paid by an Indian for a particularly attractive girl whom he planned to take with him to the various lumber camps for the purpose of gain.

With this whole matter are involved the questions of Indian barter marriages and the potlatch, customs, which the missionaries know, are united with heathenism, and which present some of the greatest difficulties to be met with in Christianizing and civilizing the Indian tribes of the coast.[20]

1906 — On the whole the Indians in this agency are inclined to be indolent and wanting in ambition according to the white man's standard. They are all very anxious to be called great chiefs, but do not care to work with their hands to accomplish this. My own opinion of the matter is that they get their food so easily that the "spur of necessity" has never been applied to them. With exception of "potlatching" and the use of intoxicants they are fairly law-abiding. Two murders have been committed within this agency. They are nearly all more or less inclined to commit perjury when questioned in a court of law, . . .[21]

1907 — The past year, though only of nine months duration, has been a banner year so far as earning power of the Indians is concerned. . . . In morality there has been a decided gain, and if the baneful influence of the "potlatch" could only be got rid of, the Indians would advance rapidly. They are beginning to awake to the fact that they must conform more and more to the white man's ways of living in order to keep pace with others . . . . MAMALILLIKULLA . . . As a rule they are law-abiding, and if the baneful influence of the "potlatch" were only eliminated, they would rapidly progress. A number of the younger men would gladly see it done away with, but they are in the minority both in numbers and influence. WEWAIAIKAI. . . . . The

[16] Canada. Annual Report on Indian Affairs, Pidcock, (1) pp. 363–365; (2) p. 579; (3) p. 579.

[17] *Ibid.*, 1900, p. 276.

[18] *Ibid.*, 1904, p. 256.

[19] *Ibid.*, 1905, pp. 234–236.

[20] Crosby, 1906, p. 232.

[21] Canada. Annual Report on Indian Affairs, Halliday, 1906, p. 232.

"potlatch" has a smaller hold amongst them than in the north end of the agency. KWAKEWLTH ..... This band seems to rest on the ideas of their former greatness, when their advice was asked by other tribes of the nation. At one time no feast of any importance was undertaken, and no movement of any kind was set on foot, without the advice and consent of the Kwakewlths. They feel still that they ought to be the leaders, but have not either numbers or the influence to do so, and it makes them discontented. Openly they seem to try to keep the law, with the exception of that relating to the potlatch, while in secret they foment trouble .... On the whole they are fairly industrious, and, if they would only use their talents in the right way, would be well off. ... They set the example to the system of exchanging wives. One of their men was sent to Vancouver, for trial on a charge of bigamy, but was acquitted on the ground that he had never gone through any form of marriage with either woman. This has done an incalculable lot of harm, not only to this band, but also to all others in the agency, as they contend that they have license to get as many wives as they need, or as they like, and get rid of them when they feel like it. NUMKISH ..... The influence of the "potlatch" has been so strong and has been assisted by other influences that their (the missionaries) efforts have to a large extent been nullified. A plot of land of the industrial school reserve has been surveyed into lots, and set apart for anyone who is willing to come out of the potlatch, and though every influence except that of force has been brought to bear, only a very few have responded to the call. ....[22]

1909 — The prevailing style of house is a huge shack built with split cedar boards covering a framework of great cedar logs, in most instances well dressed and often carved. ... Recently they have built smaller frame houses to sleep in, which are badly ventilated, but the rest of the living is in the big houses. These houses are wanted by them for the gatherings which they hold on every possible occasion.[23]

1910 — The people, like their dwellings, are of two distinct types. The older people who live for and follow the old potlatch customs, still exert a strong influence, and partially nullify all efforts put forth by the missionaries and others who are trying to better the conditions. Many of the younger people who have received a fair education would like to break away from this system, but its influence is very strong.....

Their chief aim is to go through life easily and get all the fun and glory they can out of it. The glory comes from giving a potlatch, the fun in doing nothing as often as possible. The only hope of improvement is through the education of the young.[24]

1911 — The apathy of the Indians themselves has a great deal to do with the decrease in population, and to the want of progress. They are careless and indifferent about anything that does not directly affect their pocketbook... The potlatch with its attendant evils keeps down any desire on the part of individuals to launch out for themselves, as they would practically ostracize themselves, until the movement became general. This requires more strength and stability of character than is common to the Indian. A more general feeling, however, towards the giving up of the potlatch seems to be prevalent.[25]

[22] *Ibid.*, Halliday, 1907, pp. 233–240. This report on the Kwakiutl is given tribe by tribe. There is evidence for every tribe of the presence of potlatching, although only four are given particular mention above.

[23] *Ibid.*, Halliday, 1909, p. 246.

[24] *Ibid.*, Halliday, 1910, pp. 234, 238.

[25] *Ibid.*, Halliday, 1911, p. 221.

1911 — The potlatch and its ramifications is the great stumbling block in the way of progress. There is a general feeling growing against the loss of time incurred in these meetings, but there is no decrease in the number of potlatches held nor is its influence apparently less. Nothing short of a social revolution will entirely banish the potlatch, and until this is accomplished, it will always be a great handicap.[26]

1913 — The work amongst the Indians in this agency is on the whole discouraging. The missionaries of both the Anglican and Methodist denomination have laboured for years, and laboured faithfully but the result seems to be negative. The chief source of difficulty seems to be the apathy of the Indians themselves. They are wrapped up in their old customs to a great extent, particularly in regard to the potlatch and its ramifications. All their ideas center on the potlatch. Their buildings, more particularly, the other buildings, have been built entirely with that end in view... In these houses they can entertain their friends and give away their gifts. ... KWAWKEWLTH. – The potlatch has a great hold over the people and in this respect the Kwawkewlth rank first... KOSKEMO, KWATSINO and KLASKINO. – They do not go to the same length in the potlatch as many of the others... NIMKISH. – ... if it were not for the influence of the potlatch they would forge ahead. TANATEUK. – By the rest of the Indians the members of this band are looked upon as pariahs and of little account, but this opinion is formed from a potlatch point of view.[27]

1914–1915 — SCHOOL REPORT-KWAWKEWLTH AGENCY. – Regarding ex-pupils it is to be regretted that the results are somewhat disappointing. While there is a marked difference in the deportment and general behavior of the ex-pupils and those who have not attended schools there seems to be a lack of ambition. They seem to fall back too readily into the old habits of their forefathers. However, in this agency a great handicap exists in the potlatch. Steps have been taken to suppress this evil, and further steps are now being taken, but the old potlatch ideas are so fully and firmly rooted in their minds that it will be a matter of time to eradicate them.[28]

1920 — Charles Nowell gave a potlatch at the end of the period of mourning for his brother. He was arrested for it three months afterward, was sentenced to three months imprisonment, but was parolled after six weeks.[29]

1923 — (Under the Office of Miscellaneous and Unforseen Expenditures) A payment by the Royal Canadian Mounted Police of $1,450.50 in Compensation for "potlatche" paraphernalia surrendered by Alert Bay Indians.[30]

1936 — Charley Nowell's son-in-law sold the two coppers given to him by Charles Nowell. One of them brought 33,000 blankets, the other 25,000 and gave a potlatch with the proceeds. According to Charles Nowell the value of the blankets and other articles could be stated in Canadian money as $29,000.[31]

These materials clearly show the continuity of the Kwakiutl potlatch and the failure of the efforts made to suppress it. There were numerous difficulties in enforcing the repressive legislation directed at the potlatch. The quoted passages from the agents' reports suggest some of them. In many cases, it is clear that the agent had little real understanding

[26] *Ibid.*, 1911, p. 230.
[27] *Ibid.*, 1913, pp. 223–229.
[28] *Ibid.*, 1914–1915, p. 200.
[29] Ford, 1941, pp. 223–224.
[30] Canada. Annual Report on Indian Affairs, 1923, Pt. I, p. 60.
[31] Ford, 1941, pp. 225–226.

of what he was opposing.[32] The notion that "spending" in a potlatch was the equivalent of a profligate waste of substance which deprived children of their food, the sick of proper medicines and care, and everybody of a civilized thing called "continuous comfort" is an illustration.

Because of the size of the population and the relatively wide territory over which it was scattered, it was difficult for the agents to know what was going on. As one of the agents pointed out, . . . "To reach all villages a distance of 1,000 miles has to be traversed by water and to inspect each reserve some 400 miles must be added to this."[33] After salaries, travel was the largest item of expenditure in the financial statements of the agency from 1892 to 1906.[34] Even during the period when school and medical expenditures became relatively larger, 1906–1924, the item for travel returned to its earlier prominent position in the year 1918.[35] Even so, the agents do not seem to have been in close touch with all parts of the agency and there is no evidence that any of them had the confidence of the Kwakiutl to the extent that they were given advance information about the place and time of potlatch gatherings.

Furthermore, potlatch gatherings involved large sections of the Kwakiutl population. The law was framed in terms of the individual offender, yet the "crime" was one of which a whole people was guilty. The agents seem to have been helpless in the enforcement of the law against potlatching and their own words admitting defeat bear this out. There are few records of prosecutions for potlatching. One abortive attempt to prosecute has been given above. The biography of Charles Nowell seems to indicate that enforcement of the so-called Indian Act[36]

[32] Charles Nowell's opinion of one of the Indian agents' knowledge is apparent: "When one of the Indian agents first came to Alert Bay, he came to visit us at Fort Rupert, and he began to talk about the potlatch and say he is going to stop it, for it is no good. He says 'I know all about it. I know more than you do.' I say: 'You must be older than I am, because I have lived all my life amongst them, and I still don't know everything about it.' He says 'I've been told.' And when I ask him who tells him, it is always another white man" (Ford, 1941, p. 106).

[33] Canada. Annual Report on Indian Affairs, Pidcock, 1896.

[34] *Ibid.*, 1882–1906.

[35] *Ibid.*, 1906–1924.

[36] The 1927 version of the act reads: "Every Indian or other person who engages in or assists in celebrating or encourages either directly or indirectly another to celebrate any Indian festival, dance or other ceremony of which the giving away or paying or giving back of money, goods or articles of any sort forms a part or is a feature, whether such gift or money, goods, articles takes place before, at or after the celebration of the same, or who encourages or assists in any celebration or dance of which the wounding or mutilation of the dead or living body of any human being or animal forms a part or is a feature, is guilty of an offense and is liable on summary conviction for a term not exceeding six months and not less than two months" (Revised Statutes of Canada, 1927, Vol. II, Chap. 98, no. 140, p. 2218). The reference to "wounding or mutilation" of a body is made to a winter dance ceremonial involving the Cannibal spirit.

as it referred to potlatching was made somewhat effective around the 1920's. At this time Charles Nowell was convicted of potlatching and received a three months jail sentence of which he actually served six weeks. This punishment certainly brought about no reform in his case; as his biographer says: "Despite the condemnation of the potlatch by missionary and Indian agent alike, Charley believes it to be a legitimate and honorable institution,"[37] and his actions always stemmed from such beliefs. He continued to take part in potlatches, openly where it was possible, or using special techniques of concealment where they were necessary. For him there came to be a distinction between the public or old time potlatch and the one which was given "privately." Charles Nowell shows how a "private" one was given in telling about the various potlatches he and his wife gave for their daughters:

> Beatrice was my next oldest daughter. She married Jimmy Wadhams from the Tlowitsis. He came here with his near relatives to give me the money. All came to my house. They gave me $450 to marry my daughter and $100 to Big Sam who is one of my wife's relatives. When Jimmy Wadhams want that to be paid back, I and those three will work together and pay him. The next day they went to the church and got married. Jimmy is waiting for the time when the Indian Act is amended – for the Indian Agents are promising all the time that it will be amended – so the potlatch and payment can be done in the right way. .... I gave a potlatch at her first monthly too. This was done privately – not publicly like Jane's. My wife gave the potlatch for my third daughter, Agnes, when she first got the monthly. That was done privately too. When Violet got her monthly, her mother also gave one for her that was done privately. That was done by sending people out to go around with money. One is carrying the money, and one is carrying a book where the names are written and how much is coming to them, and the one who is carrying the book tells the other how much is to be given.[38]

These "private" potlatches were a relatively late development as a means of continuing potlatching in the face of the law. It is exceptionally interesting that a written record seems to have made "private" potlatching possible, since one of the functions of publicity in this nonliterate society had always been to make important transactions like potlatch distributions a matter of record before many witnesses.[39] The Kwakiutl are also alleged to have understood and used the principle of the check for their potlatch transactions and to have gone on paying for or trafficking in the coppers deposited in the ethnological collections of the museums of North America.[40] Surreptitious potlatching was done

[37] Ford, 1941, p. 41.

[38] *Ibid.*, pp. 227–228.

[39] Boas points this out in an early description of the Kwakiutl potlatch (1898, pp. 54–55). Barnett emphasizes the dramatic and psychological functions of publicity in the potlatch as "a congregation of witnesses" (1938, pp. 349–358). These, of course, would be lost in the "private" or undercover potlatch.

[40] Bunzel, 1938, p. 359.

under necessity, but it must be noted that there seems to be an instance of a large, public traditional kind of potlatch as late as 1936.

Disapproval, legal sanctions, punishment, all failed to convince the Kwakiutl that potlatching was wrong. Charles Nowell in his later years remains serenely confident of the propriety and glory of the system he entered as a young man. He and many others, as the agency reports reveal, felt that a law as unjust and uninformed as the Indian Act would surely be repealed, and they acted accordingly. An outstanding statement of Kwakiutl pride and self-confidence in this matter was made to Boas on the occasion of his first contact with these people on their home ground. At this time Boas underwent what amounted to a public trial of his attitudes and intent as an ethnologist. He emerged with the honor of the name, Heiltsakuls or "The one who says the right things." He owed this honor, and undoubtedly the success of his work to his response to the absolutely unequivocal and uncompromising statement of the Kwakiutl position as expressed by one of their chiefs in this council:

> We want to know whether you have come to stop our dances and feasts, as the missionaries and agents who live among our neighbors try to do. We do not want to have anybody here who will interfere with our customs. We were told that a man-of-war would come if we should continue to do as our grandfathers and great grandfathers have done. But we do not mind such words. Is this the white man's land ? We are told it is the Queen's land; but no! it is mine! Where was the Queen when our God came down from heaven ? Where was the Queen when our God gave the land to my grandfather and told him, "This will be thine ?" My father owned the land and was a mighty chief; now it is mine. And when your man-of-war comes let him destroy our houses. Do you see yon woods ? Do you see yon trees ? We shall cut them down and build new houses and live as our fathers did. We will dance when our laws command us to dance, we will feast when our hearts desire to feast. Do we ask the white man, "Do as the Indian does ?" No, we do not. Why then do you ask us, "Do as the white man does ?" It is a strict law that bids us dance. It is a strict law that bids us distribute our property among our friends and neighbors. It is a good law. Let the white man observe his law, we shall observe ours. And now, if you are come to forbid us to dance, begone, if not, you will be welcome to us.[41]

Changes in Potlatching and its Expansion

The general description of the Kwakiutl potlatch given above holds good for the period from the last quarter of the nineteenth century, when detailed accounts of the Kwakiutl were first set down, to a time about fifteen years ago, when the data available in the literature are few and, when there is a strong suggestion in at least one source that the old way of life was finally losing its identity.[42] Only extensive field work at the present time could establish whether the history of the Kwakiutl potlatch is now finished. This history, however, can be ex-

[41] Boas, 1896b, p. 232.

[42] Ford, 1941, *passim*.

tended back, perhaps even as much as a century, before the time when the written record begins, and in the resulting contrast between the pre-contact and the historical materials there is evidence that certain changes in the objective features of the potlatch occurred.

TABLE 16*

The Property Distributed at Forty-Four Kwakiutl Potlatches (c. 1729—1936)

Date	No. of Potlatch	No. Woolen Blankets	No. Other Kinds of Blankets	No. of Slaves	Coppers	Trifles, "Bad Things"	Source and page
Estim. before 1729 ?	1		55	2		50 seals for feast	EK: 840
	2		50				EK: 842
	3		21				EK: 843
	4		106				EK: 844
	5		150			2 canoes, 54 dressed elk skins	EK: 845
	6		178			50 elk skins	EK: 846
	7		170				EK: 846
	8		135				EK: 848
	9		173			60 mats	EK: 849
	10		54				EK: 855
	11			2	"Moon"		EK: 856
Es. 1729	12		100	4	"Sea Lion"	4 large canoes	EK: 860
Es. 1749	13		180				EK: 863
Es. 1769	14		207				EK: 864
	15		60			40 dressed skins, 8 baskets smoked mountain goat meat	EK:1011
Es. 1789	16		170			50 seals for feast	EK: 865
	17		207			4 large canoes	EK: 865
	18		100	4		4 large canoes	EK: 869
	19		220	4		6 canoes	EK: 877
Es. 1809	20		90				EK: 875
	21		75				EK: 874
	22		160	2		2 canoes	EK:1024
	23		320	4		4 canoes	EK:1027
	24		260	6		4 canoes	EK: 881
	25		150				EK:1027
	26		100				EK:1028

* Dates that are underlined are absolutely or reasonably certain. The estimated dates are all based on family histories similar to that given in Table 17. EK refers to Boas, 1921; Daw to Dawson, 1887; F to Ford, 1941; and SO to Boas, 1895. There is some question about placing canoes with "bad things." See Table 17 for the various kinds of blankets distributed in potlatches in precontact times.

Date	No. of Pot-latch	No. Woolen Blankets	No. Other Kinds of Blan-kets	No. of Slaves	Coppers	Trifles, "Bad Things"	Source and page
	27		35				EK:1030
	28		120	4		40 elk skins	EK: 970
1849	29	20	240	4		8 canoes	EK: 882
1869	30	9,000					EK: 883
1885	31	1,000					Daw: 19
Es. 1889	32	7,000					EK: 884
	33	400					EK: 998
Before	34	5,120					EK:1113
1893	35	12,000 9,000 18,000			(3 coppers worth these amounts at their sales)		EK:1116
1894–5	36	3,400				7 canoes	SO: 346–53
1895	37	160				2000 silver bracelets	SO: 363–65
1895	38	500					SO: 579
1895	39	46				Calico for women and children 200 silver bracelets	SO: 579
	40	13,450				7000 brass bracelets 240 wash basins, spoons, abalone shells, kettles	SO: 621
1901	41	14,500				400 silver bracelets	F: 176
Between 1904—1915	42					$ 1,000 in cash	F: 205
	43	10,000					F: 205
1936	44	33,000				articles to the amount of 25,000 blankets	F: 226

An historical reconstruction of considerable reliability carries our knowledge of the processes at work in Kwakiutl culture into the pre-contact period. Eighteen Kwakiutl family histories, some of which reach back as far as twenty or more generations, are available.[43] These histories were recorded from living members of the families concerned. They are probably accurate precisely because the Kwakiutl were preoccupied with the great tradition of social positions, positions which had come down in an unbroken line of succession from their remote ancestors and had been honorably maintained by the potlatches of each successive generation. It is possible that these family histories not only maintain the relative chronological sequence of the potlatches mentioned but

[43] Boas, 1921, Vol. 2, pp. 836–1277.

TABLE 17*

A Family History of Potlatching (c. 1700—1921)

Approximate Date	Generations	Potlatchers	Property Distributed (bl–blankets)
?	I	I_2–II_1	10 sea-otter bl, 25 marten bl, 20 black bear bl, 50 seal, slaves.
		I_3–II_1	10 sea-otter bl, 30 marten bl, 10 black bear bl.
		I_2–II_1	4 sea-otter bl, 7 black bear bl.
	II	II_1–III_3	4 sea-otter bl, 10 marten bl, 7 black bear bl, 35 mink bl, 50 deer skin bl.
	III	III_8–II_1	2 canoes, 40 dressed deer skins.
		I–III	50 cedar bark bl, 50 elk skins (I_2–II_1 add 8 sea-otter bl, 50 mink bl, 70 deer skin bl.
		I_2–	10 sea-otter bl, 100 deer skin bl, 50 marten bl, 10 black bear bl.
		II_1–II_4	(for III_8). 5 sea-otter bl, 10 black bear bl, 40 marten bl, 80 deer skin bl.
		II_4–III_3	100 mountain goat bl, 9 grizzly bl, 50 elk bl, 60 mats.
		III_6–II_6	10 black bear bl, 4 marten bl, 25 elk bl, 4 lynx bl, 11 marmot bl.
		II_6–III_6	2 slaves, copper, "Moon".
	Generations IV–XII. Relationship carefully traced but no potlatches are mentioned. The question is whether this means a gap of 200 years, allowing twenty years for each generation.		
Es. 1729	XIII	XII_3–XIII_1	100 dressed skin bl, 4 slaves, 4 large canoes, copper, "Sea-Lion".
Es. 1749	XIV	XIII_3–XIV_2	100 mountain goat bl, 50 elk bl, 24 bear bl, 6 lynx bl.
Es. 1769	XV	XIII_3–XV_1	40 mountain goat bl, 25 mink bl, 30 marmot bl, 4 grizzly bl, 4 lynx bl, 4 marten bl, 100 deer bl.
Es. 1789	XVI	XIV_3–XVI_1	50 mink bl, 100 cedar bark bl, 20 sewed sea-otter bl, 50 eating seals.
		XV_1–XVI_1	2 slaves, 4 large canoes, 40 elk bl, 20 mink bl, 100 deer bl, 40 lynx bl, 7 marten bl.

* After Boas, 1921, pp. 836–885.

Estimates of dates are based on generations counted as twenty years apart. These twenty year intervals are placed with reference to two fixed points: the building of Fort Rupert in 1849 and between 1916 and 1921 when this material was recorded by Hunt from the woman XIII_1. The convergence of the fixed dates and the twenty year intervals is satisfactory for the 1849 to 1916

Approximate Date	Generations	Potlatchers	Property Distributed (bl—blankets
Es. 1809	XVII	XVII_1–XVII_2	100 mountain goat bl. 4 slaves, 4 large canoes, 100 deer bl, 40 lynx bl, 40 elk bl, 7 marten bl.
		XVI_3–XVII_2	4 slaves, 6 canoes, 60 sea-otter bl, 40 mink bl, 120 cedar bark bl.
		XVI_1	50 lynx bl, 30 marmot bl, 10 marten bl.
		XVI_1	25 marten bl, 50 lynx bl.
Es. 1829	XVIII	XVII–XVIII	6 slaves, 4 canoes, 20 bear bl, 40 mink bl, 200 cedar bark bl.
"Now the white men had come to Fort Rupert. That is the reason why . . . woolen blankets . . . . were given as a marriage gift."			
	XIX	XIX_3–XX_1	20 woolen blankets, 40 mountain goat bl, 200 cedar bark bl, 4 slaves, 8 canoes.
1849 (the date of the building of Fort Rupert)			
Es. 1869	XX	XIX_3–XX_1	Copper, "Long Top" sold by XX_1 for 9,000 woolen blankets.
Es. 1889	XXI	XX_4–XXI_2	Copper, "Sea-Lion" sold for 7,000 woolen blankets.
Es. 1909	XXII_1	Is the woman for whom the copper, "Sea-Lion" was sold. Her son, XXIII_1 was three years old when this family history was recorded between the years 1916 and 1921.	
1916–1921	XXIII_1		

also that the very dates are roughly accurate. The dates are arrived at by assigning twenty year intervals to the generations and fitting the resulting framework to the verified and fixed dates of the building of Fort Rupert and the recording of the history. Whether or not the chronology is accurate, important points of comparison and contrast are seen to exist between the pre-contact and the historical materials. Not all of the family histories are useful, since not all of them contain a reference to an event of known date; but those which do have been used in the compilation of Tables 16 and 17, which show, through time, the kinds and amounts of property distributed in Kwakiutl potlatches.

period. The dates projected backward from 1849 are probably roughly accurate, but information is lacking on the ages of the individuals involved.

Roman numerals refer to the generations and Arabic numerals to individuals within each generation. This is the identification system used by Boas and is necessary because, due to the Kwakiutl system of social positions, each individual often has several successive names in the text. The first combined Roman-Arabic figure identifies the person giving away property and the second represents the member of the family in whose name the potlatch was held. As was usual, this property was distributed to individuals outside of the family.

It is obvious from both Tables that the earliest potlatches were more modest affairs at which smaller amounts of property were distributed than was the case after the beginning of the historical record. Considering that the Kwakiutl concept of greatness in potlatching was greatness in the quantity of property distributed, it is unlikely that a Kwakiutl would ever minimize a potlatch given by one of his own ancestors, since in doing so he would be minimizing the greatness of his own potlatch position and name. Therefore, the historical reconstruction which shows relatively small potlatches for early times is no doubt factually correct.

In these two Tables there is a significant change in the amounts of property given in the pre-contact as compared with the historical period. Since blankets formed the chief article in the potlatching of both periods, we have a basis of comparison in spite of the fact that there was a change in the kind of blankets given away. A summary of the information on Table 16 shows the marked increase in the number of blankets distributed in potlatches after 1849 when Fort Rupert was built and the Kwakiutl were able to get Hudson's Bay trade blankets (see Table 18).

TABLE 18

The Greatest Potlatch in each Twenty Year Period (1849—1949)

Dates	No. of Blankets
Before 1849	320
1849–1869	9,000
1870–1889	7,000
1890–1909	18,000
1910–1929	14,000
1930–1949	33,000

Table 16 indicates that in the early period the blankets given away in potlatches in the greatest quantities were made from cedar bark and mountain goat hair or deer skins. Next to these in quantity were all the various blankets made from fur, either by utilizing the whole skin of a large animal or by sewing smaller skins together. The furs used in this manner were the fabulous sea otter, marten, black bear, elk, mink, marmot, lynx, and grizzly bear. In the early period there was apparently a distinction between the kinds of property regularly given to chiefs at a potlatch and the kind that went to "commoners." Thus, we find in one family history that in the third ascending generation six slaves, four canoes, and twenty black bear blankets were given to chiefs, while forty mink blankets and two hundred cedar bark blankets were given to commoners; in the second ascending generation just after "the white men came to Fort Rupert" four slaves, eight canoes and twenty woolen blankets went to chiefs, while two hundred cedar bark blankets and forty mountain goat blankets went to commoners; then in the latest generation the great grandson sold two coppers, one for 9,000 woolen blankets and the other for 7,000 woolen blankets, and these he distributed "to all the tribes," and apparently with no discrimination, to chiefs and commoners alike.[44]

There seems, therefore, to have been a sharp break between the pre-contact and the historical periods. The Kwakiutl shifted over completely to woolen blankets for potlatching. The reasons why they did so cannot be recreated, perhaps they found it particularly useful to have all potlatches capable of reduction to a common standard and basis of comparison one to the other, perhaps they liked sheer quantity in their potlatches and the woolen blanket could be acquired in quantities which their own methods of hunting and manufacture could never achieve for the other types of blanket. The result, however, was an almost patent illustration of Gresham's law: the cheaper, more numerous woolen blankets drove out the dearer, and scarcer blankets.

This process of substituting woolen blankets for those of fur and cedar bark started with the first known contact with the Kwakiutl on the occasion of Vancouver's stop at the Nimkish village just opposite the present location of Alert Bay. Menzies writes that some 200 sea otter skins were obtained from the Kwakiutl at this time and that:

> The articles they most esteemed were sheet Copper and coarse broad blue cloth. Of the former they took from half a sheet to two thirds for a skin, and of the latter a piece about the square of the Cloth, but they sometimes preferred Woolen Cloth made up in the form of Jackets or Trowsers.[45]

Information given by Mayne on the operations of the Hudson's Bay Company post at Fort Rupert in 1859 indicates that what was taking place was a conversion of furs to blankets. Perhaps by this date the Kwakiutl had already exchanged their fur potlatch blankets for woolen ones and were engaged in acquiring more skins to trade to the company, in any case the listing of the prices given to the Kwakiutl is highly suggestive of a direct conversion of furs to woolen blankets either at this time or somewhat earlier (see Table 19).
We know that later the Kwakiutl obtained blankets either by receiving them as wages from the Hudson's Bay Company or by converting their money wages into blankets.

Along with this sharp break in the kind of blankets used in potlatching, there occurred an even more marked break between pre-contact and historical practices in relation to the giving away of slaves at potlatches. The 1849 date marks an absolute division between the use of slaves as property to be distributed in potlatches and the absence of this practice. Table 19 reveals this practice to have been somewhat rare

[44] Boas, 1921, pp. 881–883.
[45] Newcombe, 1923.

TABLE 19[46]

Price in Blankets of Furs Traded in 1859

Skins	No.	Price Given
Bear	250	1 blanket each
Marten	2000	6 for one blanket
Mink	5000	30 for one blanket
Land Otter	250	1 blanket each
Beaver	600	2 for one blanket
Lynx	100	3 for one blanket
Fox	50	3 for one blanket
Sea Otter	50	12 blankets each

even before 1849 for it occurs in only nine of the twenty-nine potlatches. Nevertheless, it seems to have ceased altogether immediately following the first extensive contact with Europeans. Many of the reasons for this shift are discussed later in the investigation of changes in Kwakiutl winter-dance ceremonial, warfare and in the meaning of potlatching in Kwakiutl life. The data examined so far indicate a genuine expansion of potlatch activities and a standardization of them in terms of the woolen trade blanket.

A number of potlatches had to be omitted from Table 16, because information on their dates or on the amounts of property distributed was lacking. It is not possible, therefore, to measure the expansion of potlatching in terms of frequency. It is, however, possible to measure it in terms of the amount of property distributed at individual potlatches on which data are available. Taking twenty-five year periods beginning with 1850, the numbers of blankets distributed showed a marked and continuous increase (see Table 20).

TABLE 20

The Great Potlatches (1850—1940)

Date	Over 5000 Blankets	Over 10,000 Blankets	Over 20,000 Blankets
1850–1874	1		
1875–1899	3	3	
1900–1924		2	
1925–1940			2

The period which shows the greatest change is that beginning around 1875. It is of particular interest that the only historical references to an actual increase in the frequency and size of potlatches pertain to this period. There are, of course, the generalized comments of Kwakiutl

[46] Mayne, 1862, p. 185. The table as given by Mayne is reproduced only in part.

Indian agents in which their hopefulness about the eventual disappearance of the potlatch more or less cancels out their discouragement, but in the early 1880's two first hand observers record the impression that potlatching had increased at that time. The first is the report of the first Kwakiutl Indian agent, George Blenkinsop, who says "... This custom (the potlatch) has, of late years, increased to a very great extent."[47] The second is a comment by George Dawson in which he repeats Blenkinsop's opinion and states that it was shared by the Rev. Hall, who was for many years a missionary to the Kwakiutl:

> Mr. George Blenkinsop, who has been for many years among the Kwakiutl, informs me that the custom (potlatching) was formerly almost entirely confined to the recognized chiefs, but that of late years it has extended to the people generally, and become very much commoner than before. The Rev. A. J. Hall bears testimony to the same effect.[48]

This evidence taken by itself is slight, but the hypothesis of an expansion in Kwakiutl potlatching which it definitely supports is so consistent with the other facts that it acquires considerable probablility.

There were at least 658 potlatch positions in the Kwakiutl social system.[49] The earliest accurate population figure for the Kwakiutl is 2,264 for the year 1882. We do not have data on the composition of the population until the year 1898; at that time the total population is given as 1,597 and of this total 637 are listed as men of sixteen years or more in age. In other words by 1898, at least, the decline in Kwakiutl population had brought about a condition where there were more potlatch positions than men to fill them. It is reasonable to suppose that this process had been taking place since before 1882. Charles Nowell notes, although his observation cannot be dated, that "it used to be only the men and only those women that had positions that were called to go to the feasts, but nowadays all the women has their positions, because there aren't enough men alive to take the positions."[50]

An actual increase in potlatching is not only borne out by the other evidence presented in this section but also is wholly consistent with what has been presented in earlier chapters concerning the success of the Kwakiutl under the new economic conditions. That they chose to potlatch with the proceeds of their new economic achievements and that, as a result, potlatches became grander and potlatching more extensive is hardly surprising.

[47] Canada. Annual Report on Indian Affairs, 1881, p. 171.
[48] Dawson, 1887, p. 17.
[49] Boas, 1925, p. 91.
[50] Ford, 1941, p. 193.

CHAPTER FIVE

Kwakiutl Warfare

Kwakiutl warfare was not valorous. It was waged out of feelings of grief, and shame, the desire to retaliate, or, above all, to acquire or maintain the prestige of being considered utterly terrifying. It was waged on the outnumbered and the unsuspecting, on victims rather than enemies. It was ceremonialized, for the most part confined to its season, and the object of a whole expedition could be gained by one killing and the taking of a single head.[1] What actual violence occurred was dramatized superbly and outrageously. The result of this combination led to a paradox. It is reasonable to call the Kwakiutl unwarlike in character and in behavior towards Indians and Europeans alike, yet few New World groups, excepting their neighbors to the north, have been more feared.

The Kwakiutl word for war (wī'na) applied not only to fights between groups such as tribes or clans but also to acts of violence on the part of a single individual.[2] Their methods of warfare, their reasons for it and their metaphorical extension of the term to matters of marriage, supernaturalism and potlatching are better understood if *their* definition of "war" is kept in mind wherever the word is used.

A Kwakiutl war party was often made up of several great canoes carrying from thirty to fifty men apiece,[3] as many as two hundred men and sometimes more. Of these, perhaps only a few were pre-eminently warriors. The others were not thought to have any special qualities or enthusiasm for the undertaking, although they all had been through the kelp-ring ceremony which should have had the result of eliminating those who were really reluctant to accompany the expedition. In this ceremony, a piece of kelp was inflated with the breath of a man who was planning to go to war and then tied into a ring. The ring was tossed back and forth by the man and his wife, and he did not go off to fight unless the ring remained undamaged by this treatment and unless he caught it each time it was thrown to him.[4]

The warriors, however, were men whose inclinations, training, and social position fitted them to play the leading part. As was the case with

[1] Boas, n. d., pp. 1–20.

[2] *Ibid.*, p. 6.

[3] Lord, 1866, Vol. 2, pp. 256–7. In 1859 Lord saw canoes at Fort Rupert "seventy feet long, that would carry thirty fighting men over a moderately rough sea as safely as a boat."

[4] Boas, 1921, pp. 1367–72; 1895, pp. 427–428.

the Coast Salish warriors of Puget Sound,[5] they were specialists in aggression and their skills and personal qualities, although useful to their own groups at times, generally made them men surrounded and isolated by fear and dislike.

> They were taught to be cruel and treacherous and to disregard all the rules of decent social behavior. A boy who was being trained to become a warrior was treated roughly by his father who instructed him to insult and maltreat boys and to seduce girls. He was carefully trained in running, swimming, diving, and in the use of weapons of war. They strengthened themselves by bathing in very cold weather. ..He never accumulated stores of provisions. Therefore, not withstanding the property he might acquire by plunder, he could not maintain a family and many never married.
>
> Warriors walked with stiff, jerky motions, expressive of their ill humor. They must avoid laughing. Their right shoulder was always free so that they were ready for a fight. They carried stones in their hands with which they attacked people who displeased them.
>
> ...to look formidable... (They produced a profuse beard by rubbing grizzly bear blood on their faces)... and they wore the toenails of the dead suspended from their necklaces.[6]

The Kwakiutl thought that the grizzly bear possessed the qualities and powers of the ideal warrior. A warrior's prayer to the grizzly reveals these to be: the "power of not respecting anything," "of not being afraid," "wildness," or "wild hands ... that there may be nothing that is not massacred," and the "power of killing things before he is struck."[7] Men who had trained for and attempted to live up to such qualities as these were the warriors. Often they were the younger brothers of chiefs. Each Kwakiutl village had one or several such men and they were always ready for physical violence in the defense, in the attack, and even against members of their own groups.

Kwakiutl weapons consisted of bows and arrows, spears, slings, and clubs. Guns were added to this list sometime between 1785, when they were first introduced to the Indians of Vancouver Island,[8] and 1792 when Vancouver saw them among the Nimkish Kwakiutl of Alert Bay.[9] Curtis states that most of them were well supplied with guns by 1846.[10] Body armor made of wooden slats was part of war equipment[11] and the great war canoes were charred and rubbed with tallow and carried into the water, not dragged over the rough gravel,[12] in order that they would be especially smooth-bottomed and swift.

The fighting season was from about the middle of August to the first of October. At this time the water was likely to be smooth and the weather foggy, conditions which were ideal for the typical quick surprise

[5] Smith, 1940, p. 50.

[6] Boas, n. d., pp. 2–4.

[7] Boas, 1930, pp. 194–195.

[8] Curtis, E. S., Vol. X, 1915, p. 98.

[9] *Ibid.*

[10] *Ibid.*

[11] Newcombe, 1923, p. 88.

[12] Boas, n. d., p. 1.

raid.[13] Also, at this time, villagers customarily moved to a stockade or fortified site on a nearby hill or narrow inlet. If they possessed no fortifications they took to the roofs of their large frame houses at night, drawing ladders up after them.[14]

The details of the narratives of Kwakiutl warfare show its character better than any generalized description. Omitting the accounts of Lekwiltok Kwakiutl warfare and depredations,[15] there are seven reasonably full accounts dating from the time when guns were not known to some Kwakiutl groups and very scarce among the others, probably not before 1792, to 1865. Three of them make up a sequential history of raids and retaliations beginning in 1860.

In all of these accounts Kwakiutl methods of war are those of surprise, ambush, and trickery. The only instance in which there is any use of open tactics, is one in which they are only used to maximize the effectiveness of a trick. The Qagyuhl Kueha decided to war upon the powerful Quauaenok, another Kwakiutl group. Their first move was to procure the "magical death-dealing instrument that makes a noise and throws a ball through a man." This they borrowed, from a non-Kwakiutl group, the Bella Bella, at the price of one slave for a single charge of powder, one slave for a single ball, one slave for the priming powder, and one slave for the use of the gun. The Bella Bella taught them how to use this novel weapon and to prepare one of their canoes with a hole bored through the bow through which to fire it. The attackers then camped quite openly only a few hundred yards from the enemy village the night before they planned to fight and the next morning they drew up their canoes in front of the village, calling out challenges and pushing their chief's gun-canoe out ahead of the rest. The Guauaenok chief armed with his spear came out to meet the lead canoe and was shot. The war ended when his people ran back in amazed fright and the attacking chief took the body in his canoe and returned home in triumph.[16]

Other surprise tactics are numerous and varied. People are stabbed or beheaded in their sleep.[17] Ambushes are prepared where the attackers and their canoes are concealed in the deep woods at the edge of the shore[18] or where some of the attacking party dress as women and pose about a fire as though they were travellers resting and drying themselves.[19] Captives are taken and forced to pilot the war party in strange

[13] Boas, 1921, pp. 1369–1371.

[14] Boas, 1910, p. 103; Lord, 1866, p. 158.

[15] It is probably more accurate to make an exception of the Lekwiltok in such a discussion. Their warfare will be discussed later and compared to that of the main and dominant Kwakiutl type.

[16] Curtis, 1915, pp. 114–115.

[17] *Ibid.*, p. 117; Boas, 1921, p. 1374.

[18] Curtis, 1915, pp. 116, 118, 119.

[19] *Ibid.*, p. 116.

waters, to give information on the location of villages, and the best means to approach them, and even to call out in the language of the territory and lure some small party of canoers close enough to shore to make easy targets for the hidden gun-men.[20] In one case, a large canoe is split lengthwise into three long pieces so that it is possible to take it across the divide on Vancouver Island and to attack the Nootka.[21] In another case, three Kwakiutl men go to a Kwakiutl village, are hospitably fed and then shoot down their hosts after bringing their guns inside ostensibly because they want to examine them to see if the wetting they had received on the rough canoe trip had been damaging.[22]

Considering the nature of these methods of waging war it is not surprising to read in their mythology of such supernatural weapons as a sleep-bringer and a death-bringer. If the sleep-bringer were pointed at a village all its inhabitants would fall into a deep and helpless sleep; slaves and plunder could be taken without any bother, and then the attackers could draw off from the shore, point the death-bringer and cause all the village and its people to be consumed by fire.[23] These supernatural weapons involved methods which epitomize those of Kwakiutl warfare.

The character given to Kwakiutl warfare because of the use of such methods as those described was one of great ferocity in spite of the fact that the number of people killed was not large. The Kwakiutl liked to be considered ferocious and felt that such a reputation was to be gained not by widespread, frequent and exterminative wars but by the use of these dramatically vicious methods. An illuminating example can be found in the tale of the murder of a Lekwiltok warrior by the men of another Kwakiutl group who thought that he had no right to make demands of them under threat of violence:

> Now it was the desire of all the tribes to win the most terrible name for bloodthirstiness, and after Kesina was dead it was debated how they should dispose of his body so as to give themselves a great name. One proposed that they roast him, and that the smoke spreading over the earth, would carry their name with it; but the objection was offered that this would not go far enough. In the end it was decided to tie a rope around his neck and leave him lying in the water like a salmon being kept alive for food. It was then that they adopted the name Tlaalius ("the angry ones").[24]

The narratives show the most frequent reason for war to have been the desire to answer death with death. The shame, insult and loss felt at the death of a relative either by murder, sickness or accident had to be wiped out by the death of those whose rank fitted them "to die with those who are dead."[25] So rigid a balance sheet of deaths was made that the killing of several people of lesser rank would equalize the death of a

[20] *Ibid.*, pp. 115, 118, 119.
[21] *Ibid.*, pp. 120–121.
[22] Boas, 1921, pp. 1382–1385.
[23] Boas, 1910, pp. 183–187.
[24] Curtis, 1915, p. 123.
[25] Boas, 1921, p. 1385.

person of high rank;[26] and, on the other hand, a comparatively destructive act of war might fail to strike the balance: "Though they had killed ten and lost only three they had suffered a defeat because one of their dead was their leader and they had failed to bring away his body."[27]

This balance was not for the accomplishment of justice or revenge. Except for the rank of the victim it was not important whether he was a relative or even a member of the same tribe as those who had committed some act of violence previously. This is especially clear in cases where killings were made because of deaths through accident or sickness, for there is no idea that these killings were of persons who had caused the deaths in any way. There are also cases where a retaliative raid on the Tsimshian is diverted and ends with the successful killing of two Bella Bella men[28] or a war on the Bella Coola in retaliation for killings and the loss of winter dances is successfully concluded when Bella Bella men are killed and their winter dances are taken![29]

Part of the explanation for these shifts in the objectives of a war party can be found in the rule that the warriors had to return in four days, or, if the place they wanted to raid was much farther, eight days. Their type of surprise warfare required favorable opportunities and when these did not present themselves the members of the war party became anxious about the expedition and willing to attack anyone and take heads in order to bring it to an honorable conclusion. The more basic explanation, however, is that the death of anyone outside the local group could cancel out the effects of the death of one of its own members. The reasons for this need additional investigation but this undiscriminating warfare is the case to such an extent that we find in one report . . . "even if they should be relatives, they do not take mercy on them in war. They would kill whomever they might see paddling by in a canoe. Therefore, no member of the tribe goes out paddling when they know that warriors are traveling about."[30] There is an extreme instance of killing in order to "let someone else wail" on the occasion of the accidental drowning of three of the chief's relatives. A more ordinary case would be the response of a Nakoaktok man to the capture of his brother by some unknown northern group in 1860: he "determined to go fighting and to attack whomever he should meet."[31]

A second group of reasons for waging war was to acquire certain social positions, and the crests and prerogatives associated with them. Wars for such reasons seem to have been mostly internecine or waged against such near neighbors as the Bella Bella or the Bella Coola. The ranked positions of the potlatch system were accompanied by rank in the winter dance organization, forming a second series of ranked posi-

[26] Boas, n. d. p. 6; 1921, pp. 1363–1374.
[27] Curtis, 1915, p. 118.
[28] *Ibid.*, pp. 118–119.
[29] Boas, 1895, pp. 426–436.
[30] Boas, 1921, p. 1375.
[31] Curtis, 1915, p. 115.

some of the important functions of war in the two societies. These relate to what Smith has termed the Plains mourning-war complex where "There was a definite connection between mourning and war" and "the emotions of grief, anger and shame which the former excited were allayed by social recognition of success in the latter."[52] Kwakiutl head hunting, like Plains scalping, took much of its meaning from fundamental ideas that death was an attack that had to be countered. If the word "head" is substituted for "scalp," the following conclusion about this aspect of Plains warfare would fit the Kwakiutl equally well:

> The connection between the death of an enemy and the death of a tribal member, and the role of the scalp as intermediate between the two, cannot be avoided.[53]

Smith suggests that the mourning-war complex may be an underlying New World complex, and although she does not extend her study to cultures west of the Rockies, this close parallel of Plains and Kwakiutl, in spite of fundamental differences in other aspects of their warfare, indicates that this view may be correct.

In summarizing the characteristics of Kwakiutl warfare as they have appeared in the descriptive and comparative materials, it is useful to underline, first, the features Kwakiutl warfare did not possess, since without exception these prove to be ones which members of our culture habitually associate with war: Kwakiutl wars were not national; no more than a few of the local Kwakiutl groups ever banded together to wage a war; and wars were often internecine. Just as wars did not take their origin or character from any condition of national unity, they did not contribute to political or social cohesiveness. Kwakiutl wars had no significant element of economic motivation and their outcome did not deprive the vanquished of economic benefits or confer them on the victor. Bravery, as this word is ordinarily understood, had little or no part in Kwakiutl war. It is neither evident in their methods of war nor among the virtues to which they gave any general social recognition. Probably as a consequence of all of these factors, Kwakiutl war was not particularly destructive of either life or property. In spite of all the show and panoply, a single head could satisfy the purposes of an expedition of more than a hundred men.

To summarize the characteristics of Kwakiutl warfare in a more positive way, its methods were designed to be terrifying, "to win the most terrible name for blood thirstiness." It was to this end that large war parties overwhelmed a few sleeping campers or lay in ambush for two berry pickers. Heads were taken and tied to tall poles in front of the villages of the victors for the same reason.[54] Men went into ecstasies at the taking of a head and the description of the winter dance ceremonial will show how much of this was an exaggerated dramatization of the

[52] *Ibid.*, p. 461. [53] *Ibid.*, p. 460. [54] Lord, 1866, Vol. I, p. 171.

small amount of physical violence that had occurred. There is no question but that they succeeded in impressing themselves and one another with their terribleness. In one case, when two men were ambushed by a large war party both dropped dead at the first volley and afterward it was found that one had not been struck at all but had died of fright.[55]

The key to the reasons for their warfare and to its character is to be found in their preoccupation with social prestige. Some wars were fought in order to acquire crests and prerogatives that would bring prestige, some were fought in order to wipe out the shame or insult that came because of the death of relatives and consequently challenged prestige, and all wars can be considered opportunities of acquiring and maintaining the prestige of being, as Boas says, "atrocious:"

> The leading motive of their lives is the limitless pursuit of gaining social prestige and of holding on to what has been gained, and the intense feeling of shame and inferiority if even the slightest part of prestige has been lost. This is manifest not only in the attempts to attain a coveted high position, but equally in the endeavor to be considered the most atrocious member of the tribe. Rank and wealth are valued most highly, but there are also cases of criminals (in the sense of the culture we are discussing) who vie with each other in committing atrocities.[56]

Warfare and the Winter Dance Ceremonial

Warfare was one means of winning a terrible name but the main vehicle for the dramatization of this "atrociousness," or better, the greatness inherent in dealings with the terrible was the winter dance ceremonial. Competition in this sphere was not open to all any more than it was in the "profane" or potlatching sphere. The scheme of social organization was entirely different during the season of the winter ceremonial but the underlying principle of ranked positions claimed primarily through kinship and hereditary connections, and necessarily validated by distributions of property, remained. In fact, only those who had high positions in the potlatch organization had the proper claims to membership in the secret societies of the winter dance and were wealthy enough to give the potlatches which validated membership. The intricacies of this second scheme of social organization, and of the elaborate ceremonial associated with it, cannot concern us here. They make up the larger part of Boas' lengthy study on *The Social Organization and Secret Societies of the Kwakiutl Indians*[57] and form one of the fullest expositions of such materials in the ethnological literature. Our concern is with Boas' conclusion that the secret societies of the winter dance ceremonial had their origin in warfare and that the two phenomena were closely connected in practice and spirit:

[55] Curtis, 1915, p. 119. [56] Boas, 1897. [57] Boas, 1938, p. 685.

> There are, however, indications which allow us to conclude that these customs had their origin in methods of warfare. First of all, the deity, Wīna'lag·ilîs is considered the bringer of the ceremonial. This name means "the one who makes war upon the whole world", and he rules the mind of man at the time of war as well as during the period of activity of the secret societies. For this reason, also, the secret societies are in action during times of war, in winter as well as in summer. All the oldest songs of these societies have reference to war: the cannibal, the bear dancer, and the fool dancer, are considered chief warriors, and fall into ecstacies as soon as they have killed an enemy. All this seems to indicate that the origin of the secret societies has a close connection with warfare.[58]

This conclusion can be illustrated by describing the character of the various supernatural beings including Wīna'lag·ilîs, who is mentioned by Boas, the details of the costumes used in the winter dance or the performances of the ceremonials themselves. Nothing, however, conveys the extent to which the winter dances celebrated and dramatized war, more economically than the texts of some of the songs sung in the course of the ceremonies:

> Wa! Everybody is afraid of the t'sēts'aēqa mask of BaxbakuālanuXsī' waē.
> Wa! Everybody is afraid of the cannibal mask of Qoā' qoaXualanuaXsī' waē.
> His hooked-beak mask caused fluttering of the heart.
> His hō' Xhoku head mask causes fluttering of the heart.[59]

> Go on! go on! you great one! Do you not see the curdled blood on the water, the blood on the water of the many foes whom I killed and cut to pieces? I shall be the greatest nū' LmaL.[60]

> I was a little too late to witness the blood of his victims, to see the putrid heap of those whom he had killed, to see the remains of the food of the warrior of the world.
> He was made great; he was made wild by his father. He will not take pity. He will kill. He comes to make poor the tribes.[61]

> You are swooping down from heaven pouncing upon a whole tribe.
> You are swooping down from heaven, burning villages, killing everything before you, and the remains of the tribes are like the rest of your food, great thunder bird: great thunderer of our world.
> You are swooping down from heaven, going from one tribe to the other. You seize with your talons the chiefs of the tribes.[62]

> I went all around the world to find food.
> I went all around the world to find human flesh.
> I went all around the world to find human heads.
> I went all around the world to find human corpses.[63]

> Ha! The great madness came down and is disturbing our friend.
> (Nū'LmaL says:) "The weapon flew into my hands with which I am cutting off the heads."
> Ha! The great madness entered our friend and he is killing old and young.[64]

[58] *Ibid.*, p. 664. [59] *Ibid.*, p. 447. [60] *Ibid.*, p. 470. [61] *Ibid.*, p. 479.
[62] *Ibid.*, p. 476. [63] *Ibid.*, p. 459. [64] *Ibid.*, p. 471.

The connections between war and the winter dance are still not fully detailed even when it is understood that everything associated with the ceremonials is imbued with the spirit of these songs which so exaggerate and thrill at the terror and destructiveness of war. Many of the important ceremonies and concepts of the winter dance of the Kwakiutl were obtained in actual wars. It must be remembered that the man who killed another in war had the right to take the victim's names, positions, crests, and privileges for his own use.[65] That this was the object and the result of many wars explains in some measure the methods which were used, the willingness of warriors to change plans and take whatever suitable victims were presented to them, the speedy conclusion of many wars following a killing and the relatively small loss of life. In spite of the fact that the songs speak of many foes, heaps of victims, pouncing on a whole tribe, and going all around the world to find human heads, Kwakiutl warfare was waged with considerable care and restraint.

Two winter dance songs collected by Boas in 1895 make direct reference to the singer's having obtained his privileges by killing their former owners. One of them was said to have been composed about eighty years before, which would date it approximately as 1815.[66] The second had not only been obtained by killing but it is stated that its owner in 1895 was later killed and that the song and ceremony were then repossessed by a member of the group to which its original owner had belonged.[67]

It was a matter of prestige for whole divisions of the Kwakiutl whether some of their members possessed certain winter dances including the secret society memberships and all the associated songs, dances, costumes and ceremonies. Dances could be acquired by either peaceful or violent means. Marriages between the Kwakiutl tribes or even between Kwakiutl and Bella Bella could effect this peaceably, for the man customarily received the winter dance privileges of his father-in-law, in order that they might be passed on in turn to the son born into the lineage. Such peaceable means of transfer were, however, sometimes bypassed or their use was prevented by the jealous desire to keep privileges within the group or, at least, to deny them to those who were considered to be inferior. We read of how one whole tribe of Kwakiutl lacked possession of the highest ranking dance, the *hā' mats'a* or cannibal dance, and of how they finally obtained it:

> Formerly the Mā'tîlpē had no ha'mats'a, but only ha'mshamtsEs, and the other tribes would not allow them to be obtained through marriage. At one time a canoe of northern tribes passed near the village of the Mā'tîlpē. Two young men observed it, and they saw that there were four men and two women in the canoe, one of whom wore the badges of the hā'mats'a. Then the two Mā'tîlpē youths determined to kill the hā́mats'a in order to obtain

[65] *Ibid.*, p. 424. [66] *Ibid.*, p. 459. [67] *Ibid.*, p. 461.

> his dance. They paddled up to the strangers, who asked the two young men to direct them to a camping place. They did so. Then they hid their guns in the bushes nearby and told the strangers that they were on their way to look after their traps. They asked for the loan of the strangers' guns. When they had received them, they went to the place where they had hidden their own weapons, loaded them and shot the four men and the two women. One of the youths took the cedar bark ornaments of the hā'mats'a. He found his whistles in a bag. At once he began to utter the hā'mats'a cry "hap, hap" for now he had the right to use the dance owned by the man whom he had killed.[68]

It is stated by Boas, on the basis of "the testimony of all the older Indians," that the entire *hā' mats'a* ceremonial, which was the most important and highest ranking of all the Kwakiutl winter dances by 1895, was lacking among them until about 1835 when they obtained it in war from the Bella Bella or Heilsuq.[69] The account of this war details how it began as a war of retaliation against the Bella Coola who had made a destructive raid on a Kwakiutl village that contained, at the time, visitors from several other Kwakiutl tribes. All the Kwakiutl involved, Mamalelequala, Nimkish, Lauitsis, Tsawatenox and the four divisions living at Fort Rupert sent thirty-six canoes of warriors. A modest estimate of fifteen men to each canoe would mean a party of over five hundred men. One of the objects of the raiders was to get back the winter dances that had been lost to the Bella Coola. They started out after having gone through the proper ceremonies, but they had only been gone one day and night when "the warriors became sorry" that they had met no victims. One of the chiefs then proposed that they abandon their original object and "play with Awík·enox" to "gladden his heart..." While this plan was being discussed, the scout canoes of the fleet signalled the presence of travelers and soon the whole group began to draw up to six canoes of Bella Bella (Heiltsuq) which included all their chiefs. After an exchange of civilities in which the Heiltsuq chiefs were introduced and two of them demonstrated some winter dance paraphernalia including some *hā' mats'a* whistles, the Kwakiutl assured them that they would "rival with" them only in dances and that they were warring against the Bella Coola. At this point the same hot-headed chief who had previously suggested a diversion came up to the group and straightway speared one of the Bella Bella. The Kwakiutl then fell upon them and killed every one. It was decided that they had "done a great thing" and that success and prudence suggested that they abandon the Bella Coola project and go home. Every one of the Bella Bella chiefs was a *hā' mats'a* and the accounts conclude: "Since that time the tribes have the cedar bark ornaments of the Heiltsuq and their names. They obtained them by spilling the blood of these men in war."[70]

[68] Boas, 1897, p. 424.

[69] *Ibid.*, pp. 426, 664.

[70] *Ibid.*, pp. 426–430. There is a contradiction in the account. It is stated that all the Bella Bella chiefs were killed, but it is also said that one was taken as a slave.

As a result of this war the version of the *hā' mats'a* ceremonial which involved cannibalism came into Kwakiutl. Previously, the Kwakiutl had only the *hā' mats'a* in which the cannibal took hold of the heads of slain enemies with his teeth. Afterwards they had other forms of the ceremony in which a slave was killed and pieces of his flesh were torn off and eaten by the cannibals, or the cannibal bit off and ate, or pretended to eat, pieces of flesh from spectators at the festivals, or bit pieces from a mummified corpse.[71] It must be understood that such practices as these were the climaxes of their most elaborate and lengthy ceremonials and that it was precisely because they were "atrocious" and horrifying to the Kwakiutl themselves that they had such dramatic effect.[72]

Some knowledge of the winter dance ceremonial is, therefore, necessary for an understanding of Kwakiutl warfare. The unusual and unique features of Kwakiutl warfare, the absence of any real element of contest, the head hunting, the similarity between the deeds and aims of enormous war parties and single individuals, and the value placed upon a reputation for terribleness all relate to the coexistent winter dance ceremonial. The chief characteristic of the winter dance, aside from its being a large and absorbing part of Kwakiutl life, is that it did dramatize and make imaginative play with what were to them the horrors of physical violence. In both war and winter dancing, the Kwakiutl made much show with very little and invested violence with everything that would make for an overwhelmingly effective and sure-fire dramatic performance. Warfare was also often subordinate to the winter ceremonial.

History of Kwakiutl Warfare

Kwakiutl warfare ceased to exist after 1865, in marked contrast to the continuous presence and importance of the potlatch. The elimination of warfare was a major cultural change which can be explained, first, by the presence of certain tendencies in Kwakiutl life and, second, by the new contact conditions which furthered these tendencies. For example, the Kwakiutl tendency to dramatize physical violence had by 1835 brought about the acceptance of a form of the cannibal ceremony which involved no killing of an enemy or slave and no wounding, however formalized and carefully done, of the participant witnesses of the ceremony; it was considered equally effective for a mummified corpse of one of their own group to be used. As for the factor of contact, the

[71] *Ibid.*, p. 664.

[72] Boas, 1938, p. 685. See also Benedict, 1934, pp. 173–222, and Boas, 1897, p. 459, where the cannibal sings:

Now I am going to eat.
My face is ghastly pale.
I shall eat what is given to me by BaxbakuālanuXsīwaē.

Europeans of the area were quick to punish any acts of violence on a scale that was intended to teach a lesson and enforce European ideas about law and order in an absolute way. The combination of both these factors had much to do with the elimination of war, although the situation cannot be understood apart from its context and especially apart from the meaning and the place of potlatching in Kwakiutl life.

The character of much of the material that has to be included when giving a history of Kwakiutl warfare is the best possible argument for their unwarlike qualities. Many of the episodes can only be called war on the grounds that they fit the Kwakiutl definition of the word, but it must be remembered that if their definition were applied to our society it would include not only our great organized destructions but also every act of violence on the part of an individual or small group.[73] Also, apart from the violent incidents connected with the early maritime fur trade the history of all the groups of the area, including the Kwakiutl, was a remarkably peaceful one and it would not be accurate to imply that the Kwakiutl were unique except in the particular factors that caused their abandonment of war.

The Kwakiutl seem to have played a very small part in the troubled events of the early maritime fur trade on the Northwest Coast which was notorious for the violence done to the Indians by exigent and avaricious traders and the violences done by the Indians in reprisal.[74] The fur traders of the 1780's were guilty of such practices as turning their guns on nearby canoes, imprisoning chiefs for a ransom of furs, or tying them in front of the muzzles of cannon to force them to order all their people to bring their furs to trade.[75] At the time of Vancouver's visit to the Kwakiutl in 1792, the openness and courtliness of their behavior would seem to indicate that they had had none of these unfortunate experiences at the hands of the traders and had heard nothing about the conduct that could be expected.[76] It is likely that the Kwakiutl geographical position on the extreme tip of Vancouver Island and for the most part on the shores of the channel separating the island from

[73] Curtis, 1915, p. 106. Curtis gives as an example "of their method of warring upon white men" the case of the destruction of the schooner *Seabird* and its crew in 1889. A young Lekwiltok woman boarded the vessel for whiskey, became partially drunk, and was locked up below. Her husband came aboard but the crew refused to release the woman who was screaming for help. The husband returned to the boat with his brother. The crew still refused to release the woman and shot him when he took an ax to the hatch. The two Indians then attacked and killed the crew and the ship was plundered and burnt by the nearby Lekwiltok villagers. To call such an incident "war" seems to misrepresent the people, yet many of the instances of violence are like this one.

[74] Howay, 1925, pp. 387–309.

[75] Howay, Sage and Angus, 1942, p. 378.

[76] A New Vancouver Journal, *Washington Historical Quarterly*, Vol. V, No. 3 and Vol. VI, No. 1, 1915; Newcombe, 1923; Vancouver, 1798.

the mainland did make them relatively inaccessible or unknown to the sea traders.[77] George Dawson, who did some of the first ethnological work among the Kwakiutl, was of the opinion that the Kwakiutl of the village of Newettee were responsible for one of the most famous of all the violent episodes of the early maritime trade, the destruction of the *Tonquin* in 1811.[78] The evidence, however, is so incomplete that no decision on the matter is possible.

Following the events of the early maritime trade, there is record of some troubles among the Indians and of difficulties the Hudson's Bay Company men met in the Kwakiutl area. One of the most famous wars in the history of the Kwakiutl and the one previously described as the source of the modern Kwakiutl version of the cannibal ceremony occurred about the year 1835.[79] In 1838 Douglas wrote to the officials of the Hudson's Bay Company that the company profits were small principally because the Kwakiutl of Newittee were engaged in war all summer with the "Sebassa tribe, in consequence of which their time was occupied in plans of defense and revenge." He gives little evidence, however, that he considers the Kwakiutl to be destructive of anything save his profits, for in the next parapraph he notes that the company has stopped selling guns and ammunition to the Kwakiutl, not for the reasons one might suspect, but because the company had no competition at the time except from the Kwakiutl themselves who were busy peddling these articles and underselling the company in the vicinity of Fort Langley.[80]

Shortly after this time there was a controversy within the Hudson's Bay Company about the advantages of maintaining a company steamship. Of course the discussion revolved around the relation of costs to the profits to be derived directly from the use of the vessel or indirectly from the "ultimate suppression of all competition." As a secondary argument, the object of the steamer was to be "the effect produced on the natives of the Coast, whose treacherous and aggressive spirit is overawed by the exhibition of a power, which they cannot comprehend, but which they know to be irresistible."[81] It seems, therefore, that questions about the peaceableness of the Indians were not only secondary but could be solved by the awful spectacle of a steamboat! There is as a matter of fact no record of any disturbance of the peace of the area from 1837 until 1850 when a group of Nimkish Kwakiutl made a brief and unsuccessful foray into Nootka territory. This incident followed the death of the daughter of the Nimkish chief and was a typical head-hunting expedition in order to get someone "to die with those who are dead."

[77] Wike, Ms.
[78] Dawson, 1887, p. 8.
[79] Boas, 1897, p. 426.
[80] The Fort Vancouver Letters (1825–1839), p. 244.
[81] *Ibid.*, p. xxi.

In 1851 came the famous Indian troubles with the Kwakiutl of Newettee and Fort Rupert. These troubles were of a sort which not even the presence of the first governor of British Columbia and two of her majesty's gun boats could dignify as true outbreak or war. They could not even be called war according to the Kwakiutl definition, although the Indians were punished for their part in the affair on a scale appropriate to a far greater crime than the one they had committed. Three sailors from a Hudson's Bay Company vessel deserted at Victoria to a ship which was bound for San Francisco and all the attractions of the California gold fields. The ship stopped at Fort Rupert, however, for coal; the men took to the woods and were murdered by the Kwakiutl of Newettee before the Kwakiutl who had been sent to bring them back to Fort Rupert could catch up with them. When the bodies were brought back to Fort Rupert all the white miners and other workers stopped work, hid in the woods, and waited for a chance to board the ship bound for the gold fields, passing the time apparently with the help of liquor they had procured from the ship and justifying their action on the grounds that the Company had ordered the Indians to murder the deserters.

Governor Blanchard and the two gun boats arrived on the scene about a month after the incident had begun with the desertions in Victoria and the Governor's specially appointed magistrate set out for Newettee to demand the surrender of the murderers. The Indians refused this demand and their offer to pay damages in furs and blankets was refused in return. One of the gun boats was then sent to Newettee. The village was found to be deserted and was destroyed.

The following year a gun boat was again sent to Newettee to settle the matter or to deal out more punishment. There was a skirmish during which two Indians were killed and several sailors were wounded before all the Indians took to the woods. Their new village located on a different site was then fired upon and destroyed. Shortly after this a reward for the murderers was offered and the affair was concluded when their bodies were brought to Fort Rupert, even though there was considerable doubt as to whether the bodies were indeed those of the murderers or whether a slave had been killed to make up the proper total.[82]

The literature makes no reference to any further difficulties with any branch of the Kwakiutl until 1858 when Mayne states that the "U-cle-ta" (Lekwiltok), "the Ismailites of the country," had fought with the men of some northern tribe coming south through their territory.[83]

These materials on warfare are so intermittently spaced in time and reveal the Kwakiutl to be on the whole so peaceful a people that the number of events occurring in 1860 is surprising if the genuinely unwarlike character of many of them is not. At this time, the Lekwiltok

[82] Dawson, 1887, p. 10; Short and Doughty, 1914, Pt. I, pp. 92–95.

[83] Mayne, 1862, p. 73.

attacked and robbed a party of Chinese. They were punished by the usual method of having a government frigate sent to fire upon their village and they restored the stolen property after several of their men had been killed. In this same year, the Nakoaktok Kwakiutl killed seven Tsimshian on one war raid and ten Tsimshian on another. Probably also in 1860, although the date is not quite certain, some of the Kwakiutl of Fort Rupert became embroiled with the southern Indians on their return from Victoria. One of the Kwakiutl chiefs was murdered by a Songhie Indian on their departure from Victoria. The Kwakiutl then had a brush with the Indians of Nanaimo on the return trip in the course of which they captured and carried off a Nanaimo woman. One account states that they also killed several Nanaimo men.[84] In any case, the Nanaimo appealed to the authorities and the gun boat, *Daedalus*, which had figured in other disciplinary expeditions, was sent to Fort Rupert to effect the return of the captured woman. The matter was peacefully concluded after some show of resistance and considerable bargaining on the part of the Kwakiutl.[85]

Lord, one of the informants present at Fort Rupert during this incident saw evidence of another Kwakiutl raid. A scalped head had been strung up on a pole just outside the village and the Hudson's Bay men informed Lord that it was the head of a chief who had been captured with several others on a Kwakiutl raid and killed on the beach at Fort Rupert and beheaded only a few days before. Jacobsen confirms Lord's story and gives the additional information that the killing and beheading of the captive had been done in connection with the cannibal ceremony and that when the authorities learned about it they sent the usual cannon boat, demanded the surrender of the guilty participants, were refused and then destroyed all the houses and canoes in the village. Jacobsen records that only a part of the Kwakiutl population returned to rebuild their village, the rest scattering or taking up residence on the mainland, and that those remaining at Fort Rupert had lost some of their feeling of superiority and self-confidence.[86]

As a lighter note in this 1860 catalogue of disorders, Lord's examination of the Hudson's Bay Company fort at Fort Rupert revealed that its formidable and business-like appearance was "a pleasant fiction," and that its entire armament consisted of "two small rusty cannonades buried in the accumulated dust and rubbish of years" which "no human power could load."[87] The aim of the Company was to make profits, and not to eliminate, by force if necessary, those aspects of Kwakiutl life which were repugnant to Europeans. Functioning on this basis, it had no need of armament to live peacefully among a genuinely unwarlike people.

[84] *Ibid.*, p. 208.

[85] Lord, 1866, Vol. I, pp. 153–155, 166–168; Mayne, 1862, pp. 208–212.

[86] Jacobsen, 1884, pp. 50–51.

[87] Lord, 1866, pp. 163–164.

In his visit to the Kwakiutl in the 1880's Jacobsen saw a letter in the hands of a Koskimo which said that the Koskimo had murdered two sailors in 1864. The Koskimo man did not know the contents of this letter and Jacobsen notes that it was not infrequent for the Indians to possess and proudly display letters which they had been led to believe were in their praise but which were actually often unwarranted and damaging practical jokes publicizing them as scoundrels, fools or criminals. Since there is no corroboration of these murders in other sources, they may not have occurred at all.[88]

In 1865 the Kwakiutl sent a war party out against the Sanetch to the south. They attacked a group of sleeping campers, seven adults and two children, and killed all but one of them. This raid was a head-hunting raid of the classic type "to get someone to die with those who are dead," for the sister, niece and brother-in-law of a Kwakiutl chief had been killed on their way back from Victoria by the capsizing of their canoe, by strong drink, or by a combination of the two.[89]

This is the final instance of "war" in Kwakiutl life. In 1876, 1885, and 1910 there were killings which the agents claimed were committed under the influence of liquor, and there were four other killings within the period. None of these was in the old pattern of warfare or physical violence and most of them were committed by the Lekwiltok who were not a typical Kwakiutl group.

The winter dance ceremonial was to continue for another thirty years in spite of legislation which attempted to suppress it, but the last record of winter dance performances is the description given by Boas who witnessed them in 1894, 1895 and 1896 at Fort Rupert. The very extensive character of the ceremonials given at that time makes it difficult to accept the fact that they came to an end so quickly afterwards, and it seems more likely to conclude that they did not actually go out of existence but that they went underground and were held when agents were known to be in other parts of the agency or by some similar means of avoiding the authorities. Nevertheless, the absence of official reports of winter dancing after 1896 is corroborated by the biography of Charles Nowell. In 1901 his father-in-law gave him a box containing masks and ceremonial equipment and the right to give a winter ceremonial at the time he gave him the copper. In 1940 Charles Nowell, who revealed the "underground" practice of potlatching in recent years without hesitation, said "I still have my box unopened, because I haven't given a winter ceremonial yet."[90]

Thus, both warfare and winter dancing ceased to exist except in the minds and memories of the Kwakiutl, while potlatching continued to be an active and absorbing interest.

[88] Jacobsen, 1884, p. 63.

[89] Boas, 1921, pp. 1363–1380.

[90] Ford, 1941, p. 178.

CHAPTER SIX

FIGHTING WITH PROPERTY

"Fighting with property" instead of "with weapons," "wars of property" instead of "wars of blood," are Kwakiutl phrases expressing what has proved to be a fundamental historical change in Kwakiutl life occurring within the period known to history. It has been the purpose of this investigation to trace the various tendencies in Kwakiutl life as they were furthered or inhibited by the pressures of the contact culture and to determine both the binding force and the dynamics of this historical process. The general conclusion is that the binding force in Kwakiutl history was their limitless pursuit of a kind of social prestige which required continual proving to be established or maintained against rivals, and that the main shift in Kwakiutl history was from a time when success in warfare and head hunting was significant to the time when nothing counted but successful potlatching.

This conclusion about Kwakiutl history has emerged from the data and can be explained by them. That some of the Kwakiutl were aware of the historical change in their way of life gives additional confirmation as well as additional insight into the character of these people. Most of the Kwakiutl statements indicating this awareness were made within the period of the eighteen day winter dance ceremonial given at Fort Rupert in 1895.[1] The statements themselves are very explicit:

> This song which we just sang was given by the wolves to Ya'xstaL ... when he received the death bringer with which he was to burn his enemies or to transform them into stone or ashes. We are of Ya'xstaL's blood. But instead of fighting our enemies with his death bringer, we fight with these blankets and other kinds of property.[2]

> We are the Koskimo, who have never been vanquished by any tribe, neither in wars of blood nor in wars of property.. Of olden times the Kwakiutl ill treated my forefathers and fought them so that the blood ran over the ground. Now we fight with button blankets and other kinds of property, smiling at each other. Oh, how good is the new time![3]

> We used to fight with bows and arrows, with spears and guns. We robbed each other's blood. But now we fight with this here (pointing at the copper which he was holding in his hand), and if we have no coppers, we fight with canoes or blankets.[4]

[1] Boas, 1897, pp. 544–606.
[2] *Ibid.*, p. 577.
[3] *Ibid.*, pp. 580–581.
[4] *Ibid.*, p. 571.

> True is your word, . . . When I was young I have seen streams of blood shed in war. But since that time the white man came and stopped up that stream of blood with wealth. Now we are fighting with our wealth.[5]

> The time of fighting has passed. The fool dancer represents the warriors but we do not fight now with weapons: we fight with property.[6]

The Potlatch as a Kind of Fighting

Along with these statements goes a wealth of evidence demonstrating that the potlatch was considered to be a kind of fighting. The description of the potlatch given above included materials which indicated that potlatching was a metaphorical warfare, but it is necessary to show how much this was the case. Potlatches were planned like campaigns against an enemy. Although they were given by individuals, it must be remembered that the numaym and even the tribe to which the individual belonged had their prestige and rank at stake in every potlatch. Before and during a series of potlatches given in connection with the 1895 winter dances, two of the Kwakiutl groups involved, the Koskimo and the Kwakiutl of Fort Rupert, had separate meetings in the course of which strategy was planned and they were exhorted to make the most intensive efforts to win out over their rivals, or "friends on the other side." The Kwakiutl of Fort Rupert were appealed to in the following fashion:

> Friends, I ask you to keep yourselves in readiness, for the Koskimo are like to a vast mountain of wealth, from which rocks are rolling down all the time. If we do not defend ourselves, we shall be buried by their property. Behold, friends! They are dancing and making merry day after day. But we are not doing so. Remember this is our village and our battlefied. If we do not open our eyes and awake, we shall lose our high rank. Remember, Kwakiutl, we have never been vanquished by another tribe.[7]

On each of the two days following, the Kwakiutl held secret meetings again. At the first they were told . . . "the Koskimo are likely to beat us in our war with property. Therefore I ask you not be to asleep, else the Koskimo will surely walk right over us, friends!"[8] At the second, two speakers set forth reasons why they should be anxious about their potlatches with the Koskimo and should exert themselves:

> . . . O friends! Let me ask you chiefs and new chiefs of my tribe, do you wish to be laughed at by our rivals? We are almost beaten by the Koskimo. We are only one potlatch ahead of them. After this pile has been distributed, we shall only be two potlatches ahead of them, instead of four as our fathers used to be. Take care friends! Our friends the Koskimo are strong in rivalling us in distribution of property . . .

> . . . He spoke about our rivalry with the Koskimo, and said that we were beaten by them. This is true, although we are two potlatches ahead of them.

[5] *Ibid.*, p. 571.

[6] *Ibid.*, p. 601. This statement was made with reference to a dancer whose predecessor in the ceremonial position had actually killed many men in war and head hunting.

[7] *Ibid.*, p. 576.

[8] *Ibid.*, p. 582.

> You know that every time when the tribes come to our rich village, we always have four or five persons more to give blankets away than they have. Therefore, take care, young chiefs! else you will lose your high and lofty name; for our grandfathers were never beaten, neither in war of blood nor in war of wealth, and therefore all the tribes are below us Kwakiutl in rank.[9]

The speech made at a meeting of the Koskimo the next day shows that the Kwakiutl of Fort Rupert were correct in their estimate of the situation. The Koskimo were aware of their numerical advantage in potlatching but did not underestimate their potlatch enemies:

> We have two chiefs in our tribe and therefore we cannot be vanquished in our strife with property. Look out! Do not let the Kwakiutl vanquish you, for they are a few only. See how many you are! There are enough Koskimo to fill the seats all round the walls. The Kwakiutl could not fill one half the seats in this house. Therefore they cannot vanquish us. Take care friends![10]

The element of contest and the evocation of an almost patriotic fervor, both warlike features absent in their actual warfare, are present in these speeches. The strategic planning of potlatches in order to challenge or to maintain positions is present in the full account from which the quoted speeches were taken.

It would be difficult to exaggerate the degree to which the talk, the songs and the ceremonies of potlatching borrowed the metaphor of war and even developed it to the point where the metaphorical war had more meaning and thoroughness than their one time "fighting with weapons." The usual word for potlatch was "p!Esa," to flatten, and it came to mean to flatten a rival under a pile of blankets or "means of flattening," for the word for "potlatch blanket" took its origin from the same root and had this literal meaning.[11] The names of coppers often indicated that they were indeed the weapons of the new kind of warfare, potlatching: "War,"[12] "About whose possession all are quarreling,"[13] "Cause of Fear,"[14] "Means of Strife."[15] A great copper belonging to a chief was spoken of as his acropolis or fort on which he and his tribe could stand in safety and greatness.[16] A broken copper was spoken of by its owners as "lying dead in the water off our beach"[17] meaning that the breaking of it was as successful an attack against the rival as a killing would have been.

The songs sung at potlatches call upon all the imagery of war and apply it to the distribution of property! In the last song given below, the

[9] Boas, 1905a, p. 485.
[10] Boas, 1897, pp. 589–590.
[11] Boas, 1921, Part II, pp. 1402, 1441, 1447; 1910, p. 435.
[12] and [13] Boas, 1897, p. 344.
[14] and [15] Boas, 1925, pp. 171, 201.
[16] *Ibid.*, p. 147. See also, 1921, Pt. II, p. 1431.
[17] Boas, 1897, p. 564.

text speaks only of war, yet Boas was informed that every reference to war meant only the distribution of property in potlatches; that every image of war given here had its potlatch equivalent in meaning; and that the song actually commemorated a victory in potlatching by the Fort Rupert Kwakiutl over the Nimkish.

> The great Ia'k·îm will rise from below.
> He makes the sea boil, the great Ia'k·îm. We are afraid.
> He will upheave the seas, the great Ia'k·îm. We shall be afraid.
> He will throw blankets from out of the sea, the great Ia'k·îm.
> He will distribute blankets among all the tribes, the great Ia'k·îm.
> We fear him, the great Ia'k·îm.[18]

> What is on the enemies' blanket? Wiēē.
> War is on the enemies' blanket. Wiēē.[19]

> Food will be given to me, food will be given to me, because I obtained this magic treasure.
> I am swallowing food alive; I eat living men
> I swallow wealth; I swallow the wealth my father is giving away.[20]

> Let us show what we gained by war!
> . . . I did not turn my face backward to look at those who were bothering me when I went to make war on you friend.
> Throw your power that is killing everybody, throw your fire of death, throw what makes them turn their faces downward, throw it against them who went to make war upon you.
> I surpass them, they are the lowest of the whole world.
> I pulled them into my canoe to be my slaves, that they bail out the war canoe.[21]

The ceremonial, like the songs, not only takes much of its imagery from warfare but also substitutes in many cases the symbols of successful potlatches for what at an earlier time was evidence of success in real war. For instance, in the description of the Koskimo winter ceremonial of 1895 there are many such details:

> Each man carries as many hemlock wreaths as he had killed enemies during war expeditions. They also carry bows and arrows. Then they step up to the middle of the house and throw one wreath after the other into the fire, calling the name of the enemy whom it represents. As soon as a wreath is thrown into the fire they call "yē", and all repeat this cry. At the same time they shoot arrows into the fire. This ceremony is called yî'lxoa, which means placing the head of an enemy on a pole. The fire is called XusE'la which means fighting place. The whole ceremony is called al'Xts'āliL wā'lastEm (carrying blood into the house and giving away much property) or k·'ā'g·euLaxstā'la (sharp edge of a knife). At present the wreathes represent the number of coppers which a man has given away. They have taken the place of heads, because according to the usages of the Kwakiutl, a man who has given away a copper by doing so becomes a victor over his rival.[22]

[18] *Ibid.*, p. 482. Iák·îm is a sea monster and one of the spirits of the winter dance ceremonial.
[19] *Ibid.*, p. 576.
[20] *Ibid.*, p. 459.
[21] *Ibid.*, p. 485.
[22] *Ibid.*, p. 522.

9

Rivalry in which Fighting and Potlatching were Combined

Although the imagery of warfare as it was applied to potlatching seems to have more force than the actual practices of war to which it refers, there seems to have been a time when fighting with weapons and fighting with property were more or less equal and interchangeable means of gaining prestige. The use of such imagery suggests a carry-over from an earlier situation of this sort and there is additional evidence to support this view. This evidence consists of three stories of rivalry between Kwakiutl chiefs. The dating of the stories is uncertain, but they have in common a mixture of potlatching and physical violence which is not characteristic of the potlatch as it is known and described in the latter part of the nineteenth century. In spite of the fact that the stories are undated and of a traditional character, the claim made for one of them by George Hunt that "this is the true story of two chiefs"[23] might be made with full justification for his story and the other two as well.

The first story is about the origin of the Kweka group of the Kwakiutl in the violent rivalry of two brothers; the victor and survivor established the new group. Charles Nowell repeats the story his father had once told him and introduces it by saying that the Kwakiutl did not like to be reminded that the Kweka or "murderers" had once worsted them and that they were the descendants of the brother who had been killed. He adds that the Kweka only made reference to this matter "when we are fighting them with potlatches."[24] According to the story, the rivalry began when the two chiefs, Maxwa and Yakodlas, bet heavily against one another on the outcome of a throwing game their young men were playing. Yakdolas won and gave a potlatch to the tribe of Maxwa with his winnings. The story then reads "...Maxwa also gave a potlatch, and so they went on in that way. When the one give a feast, the other give a feast; when the one give a potlatch, the other give a potlatch. They begin to have hatred between them." Then Maxwa gave a feast and Yakodlas and his group noticed that one by one the men of Maxwa's group had slipped out of the house. They suspected trouble and left the house themselves holding a heavy cedar plank over the head of their chief, a wise precaution when it was seen that Maxwa had indeed posted one of his men on the roof with a great rock to throw down on Yakodlas. This open enmity continued and finally Maxwa was killed.[25]

The second is the famous story of the two rival chiefs, Fast Runner and Throw Away, both chiefs of the same village of the Kwakiutl but of different numayms. The two chiefs "who were true friends in the beginning" became involved in deadly potlatch rivalry in which Throw Away was beaten when he was unable to equal the feats of Fast Runner

[23] Hunt, 1906, pp. 108–136. [24] Ford, 1941, p. 57. [25] *Ibid.*, pp. 57–61.

in destroying a second copper, in breaking up and burning four canoes and in burning two slaves alive in connection with the winter ceremonial. Throw Away seems to have had no choice but to make a suicidal war against the Nootka. One man escaped to tell the Kwakiutl that Throw Away and the rest of his party had all been killed and the account ends: "Well, then was beaten Throw Away after that."[26]

The last of the accounts is a tradition of the Nimkish, the Kwakiutl group living at what is now called Alert Bay. It concerns the violences committed out of the desire to possess the large copper, "Causing Destitution," that was obtained originally from the Bella Bella. The fathom and a half long copper was highly prized and soon after its second owner had bought it, for ten slaves and ten canoes and ten lynx blankets, he was pursued because of it but managed to hide it in the ground before he was killed. Two orphans found it and gave it to Wa'xwid, the successor of the man who had been killed, rather than to their own uncle who had not been treating them kindly. The two men quarreled and the jealous uncle and his followers killed Wa'xwid and robbed him of all he possessed including the great copper, which was by this time worth a fabulous amount:

> ....there was nothing that was not paid for it. It made the house empty. Twenty canoes was its price; and twenty slaves was its price; and also ten coppers tied to the end was its price, and twenty lynx skins, and twenty marmot skins, and twenty sewed blankets, was its price; and twenty mink blankets was its price; and one hundred boards was its price; and forty wide planks was its price; and twenty boxes of dried berries added to it, and twenty boxes of clover, and also ten boxes of hemlock-bark, was its price; and forty boxes of grease was its price; and one hundred painted boxes was its price; and dried salmon not to be counted was its price; and two hundred cedar blankets was its price; and two hundred dishes was its price.[27]

This valuable copper which would cost even more at its next potlatch sale, was then "obtained by killing" along with other property and the names and crests of the dead owner.

There is no certainty that these traditional accounts describe early conditions accurately but the suggestion they make of the existence of a period when physical violence and potlatching were equal means of winning over rivals is consistent with the views of the Kwakiutl as to the course of their history, the great extent to which potlatching retained the phraseology and symbol of war and violence, and the actual record of historical events and developments.

[26] Hunt, 1906, pp. 108–136.
[27] Boas, 1910, pp. 83–95.

The Shift From Physical Violence to Potlatching

The historical materials have clearly detailed the continuous vigor and even growth of the potlatch until recent years, in contrast to the extinction of warfare and winter dancing in Kwakiutl life. The record of potlatching continues until about 1930 when the data become sparse and there is a doubt about its presence which can only be resolved by a field trip into the area. One of the most marked features of the historical record of the potlatch is the contrast in the size of the potlatches given before the approximate date of 1849 when a relatively small amount of property was distributed and after that date when the amount increased sharply. The winter dance ceremonial which was one of the many occasions for potlatching and which was associated with warfare in spirit and origin became extinct around the turn of the century. The last descriptions of the winter dance are dated 1895. The last war occurred in 1865 and this date must be used in connection with the facts that there is no record of any disturbance of the peace between the years 1837 and 1850, and that after 1850 the only notable breaches of the peace occurred in 1860. The date, 1865, therefore, represents an extreme limit.

These dates give the rough outline of the historical change in Kwakiutl life. When the outline is filled in with a description of the character of the Kwakiutl potlatch and Kwakiutl warfare, and especially, when it is understood that the increased vigor of potlatching and the extinction of warfare were related and simultaneous occurrences, the picture becomes well-defined. When the rivalrous character of the Kwakiutl potlatch is kept in mind, the historical shift in Kwakiutl life is tellingly expressed by their own phrases, "wars of property" instead of "wars of blood" and "fighting with wealth" instead of "with weapons."

There is an interesting question as to the possibility of dating this shift more precisely. The period within which it occurred is between the time when the white men built Fort Rupert in 1849, and the attendant increase in the size of potlatches, and the time when warfare ceased in 1865. All the materials suggest that the shift should be placed early in this period. Interest and activity in warfare seem to have been attenuated even before 1849. In one case, the end of "trouble" and the beginning of a peaceful era is definitely placed close to the year 1849. In 1895 an old man told George Hunt, "Your days, young men, are good. But our past ways were evil when we were all at war against each other. I mean you have no trouble nowadays. I was three times pursued by northern Indians at the time when we were still naked."[28] The establishment of the trading post at Fort Rupert would have brought an end to the time when the Kwakiutl "were still naked". The Kwakiutl

[28] Boas, 1897, p. 425.

also said that "the white man came and stopped up (the) stream of blood with wealth"[29] and, while it is not possible to know exactly how soon significant quantities of the white man's wealth came into Kwakiutl hands, the number of woolen trade blankets distributed at potlatches very shortly after 1849 indicates that it was early. Making due allowance for the fact that the data are not full and that there is an inherent difficulty in assigning a definite date to a cultural historical change which is essentially a development or a shift in emphasis rather than a discontinuity, this shift in Kwakiutl life seems to have occurred not long after 1849.

Summary

The historical developments in the various areas of Kwakiutl life explored by this study resulted in strengthening the potlatch and in weakening and inhibiting warfare. They can be summarized in the briefest possible form under the categories of population, economic life, warfare, and fighting with property.

Population. Kwakiutl population declined rapidly and continuously from at least 1837 to the year 1924. Since the primary cause of this decline was the infectious diseases introduced by Europeans, the decline probably started earlier than 1837, a view that is in accord with Kroeber's estimate of a dense pre-contact population in this area. Kwakiutl population was on the decline through the critical period in which the shift to fighting with property occurred and it encouraged the shift. It brought about a higher proportion of potlatch positions in relation to population which meant that, while the system of a fixed series of ranked potlatch positions remained undisturbed and solid, access to a position was easier than it had been, even reaching the point where there were more positions than individuals to fill them. It can even be presumed that younger sons or daughters, and commoners who were able to enter the system by means of some hereditary claim, however remote, would have an extra measure of enthusiasm for the potlatch and be particularly active in its support.

Economic life. The character of Kwakiutl economic life and the historical developments in this area of Kwakiutl culture constitute the most numerous and significant factors producing the shift from fighting "wars of blood" to fighting "wars of property." In general, the Kwakiutl were a people of marked economic ability who made a success in the new and expanding economy created by the Europeans in the area and who used the proceeds of this success for potlatching. Throughout the historical period observers noted that the Kwakiutl adjusted success-

[29] *Ibid.*, p. 571.

fully to the new economy, if not to the new society. Certain attitudes and practices characteristic of Kwakiutl economic life from the time of the earliest records, and presumably in pre-contact times, facilitated this adjustment. The Kwakiutl were extremely able and industrious. Their own industrial procedures and food-getting techniques were varied, specialized and concerned with production far in excess of mere need. They seemed always to have aimed at as large a storable surplus of food products as possible and at the greatest possible pluralization of manufactured objects. From the time of their earliest contacts with Europeans in business and trade, they were uniformly and continuously energetic and astute. These qualities and traditional habits were extraordinary assets in meeting the new economic conditions and in taking advantage of their expanded opportunities.

The habituation to standardized and pluralized manufactured objects was carried over into the new economic situation in their acquisition of European manufactures. One of the most interesting features of the potlatch was the distribution of great numbers of manufactured goods of the same category. In the old days, the number of objects in each category had been smaller but the principle was established for the later potlatches with their hundreds or thousands of blankets, hundreds of silver bracelets, dozens of zinc washboilers and yards of calico. The Kwakiutl had a potential demand for European goods in excess of any practical utility the goods might have possessed. This can be seen both as a stimulus to Kwakiutl integration into the new economy and as a direct stimulus to the potlatch. Their own manufacturing techniques by handicraft would have been incapable of producing the relatively cheap and impressive abundance their potlatching came to require. In other words, the Kwakiutl potlatch was encouraged by the cheap goods the industrial revolution had made available.

Developments in the occupational field were an unusual combination of sustaining traditional occupations, entering commercialized versions of old occupations, or entering new ones which possessed traditional and congenial features. They continued to earn their own subsistence, which meant that cash earnings could go into the purchase of manufactured goods. Since they required only a limited amount of manufactured goods for consumption needs and since they did not hoard, any surplus could be and was used in potlatching. They specialized and commercialized some of their own products for sale among themselves.

Already familiar with the natural resources of their land and trained in their exploitation, they were able to take an indispensable place in the commercialized fishing and lumbering industries of British Columbia. Already flexible and migratory in their occupational habits, they were used to orchestrating an economic life out of a whole series of seasonal jobs and were prepared to profit from the salmon runs, olachen runs, hop-picking seasons and many other such occupations. The fact that the Kwakiutl became in time a rather small minority in the labor force, with the influx of Whites, Japanese and Chinese into the area, and yet were still able to maintain a place in it, is a good measure of their success in the occupations of the new economy which were open to them or which they chose to enter. Their habituation to seasonal work and the fact that most of the employment opportunities in this area, whether of a subsistence or commercial character were seasonal, gave them good earnings and freed them of the necessity of economic activity during the winter months. They then had both the means and the time to potlatch.

The cash income received by the Kwakiutl is one of the best measures of their adjustment as a group to the new economic life surrounding them. Actual income figures exist only for the period beginning in 1903. The critical period of the major historical shift in their way of life to "fighting with property" had already occured by that date. The figures from 1903 on show that Kwakiutl income was sizable, when it is considered that it did not have to go for subsistence needs, and that it was increasing sharply. In spite of the fact that no figures exist for the earlier critical period of the second half of the nineteenth century, the economic data as a whole do not indicate in any way that the earnings situation of the Kwakiutl differed in this earlier period.

Whether the possibility of acquiring quantities of European goods first increased potlatching or whether the interest in potlatching first motivated the Kwakiutl to acquire the quantities of European goods they regarded as useful and impressive in potlatching, the situation was progressive and the Europeans showed much less insight into the historical process than the Kwakiutl. Members of the new culture preached and legislated ineffectually against the potlatch at the same time they praised the Kwakiutl for their industriousness and their successful adjustment to the new economic conditions. Yet Kwakiutl economic achievement was motivated by potlatching and sustained and increased potlatching! The "stream of wealth" of which the Kwakiutl speak was at once the measure of their successful integration with the new and expanding economy and the motive for their success.

Warfare. Unlike the Kwakiutl potlatch, Kwakiutl warfare was incapable of becoming an increasingly important part of Kwakiutl life; it was suppressed as a result of historical developments and it was eradicated within twenty years after the period of intensive contact with the new culture. The character and tendencies of Kwakiutl warfare, itself, helped to bring about its extinction. It was neither an area of Kwakiutl life in which particular advantages not available in other areas were to be gained nor was it a special area for the development and exhibition of "warlike" qualities highly valued by the society. Rather Kwakiutl warfare was bent to the services of a vast and intricate system of rivalry for purposes of social prestige and this rivalry had always been more fully expressed and dramatized in the potlatch.

There may have been a time when Kwakiutl warfare was not subordinated to ends which warfare, itself, did not satisfy. The record, for example, shows that in the early part of the nineteenth century certain developments of the winter dance ceremonial were at the expense of the amount of physical violence in Kwakiutl life; that as violence became increasingly ceremonialized and dramatized, instances of violence decreased in number. It is not unlikely that this was a continuation of a process begun at a much earlier time. As far back as the record goes, however, the Kwakiutl were not warlike and not interested in war as such but only as it was related to social prestige. They waged war either to make up the loss of prestige they felt at the death of a relative, or to gain new and greater prestige by killing men in possession of valued winter dance privileges and potlatch positions in order to take these honors away from them. Needless to say, these honors were of no account without the potlatching which gained them the proper publicity and recognition.

It is difficult to know to what extent the end of warfare was brought about by the punitive and disciplinary measures taken by the Europeans in the area. Certainly the Kwakiutl were overpunished for any violence that occured and certainly they soon gave up their warfare. A most interesting statement in relation to this problem was made to Boas by the Kwakiutl of Fort Rupert around the year 1895. The statement, previously quoted in full, expresses the greatest defiance about attempts to change their culture by missionizing, legal pressures or force. They said that the white man could come and raze their village to the ground, but that they would rebuild it and continue their winter dances and their potlatches. Warfare was not mentioned, since it had ceased at least thirty years before, and the winter dance ceremonial which they were defending no longer possessed such features as the killing of a slave or other acts of physical violence. In this defiant statement, they are undoubtedly referring to the punitive expedition against their village some thirty-five years before when all the houses of the village had been destroyed in punishment for the killing of a war captive in connection with a winter ceremonial. The statement seems to mean that they had been forced to abandon warfare and physical violence but that they could not be forced to give up their more cherished practices of winter dancing and potlatching. It seems likely that the use of force against them had some effect in eliminating physical violence in Kwakiutl culture. However, forces were involved in this historical development that were far more pervasive and positive in effecting a cultural change than the occasional use of military force.

Fighting with property. The cultural-historical change in Kwakiutl life occurring not long after 1849 was not merely the elimination of warfare, it was the completion of the process of domesticating warfare into the service of the all important rivalry for social prestige in which the potlatch was the principle method and test of achievement. Kwakiutl fighting in war had been for social prestige and its value had been in the dramatic additions it could make to reputations for greatness and terribleness in rivalry. The Kwakiutl potlatch, throughout the historical record, was always a form of rivalry and fighting and it could absorb and command anything in warfare that would add to its impressiveness. It was ridden with the imagery and drama and meaning of Kwakiutl warfare and it was empty of physical violence and destructiveness except occasionally towards property. The new economic situation stimulated the peaceful warfare of the potlatch and furthered the tendency already present in Kwakiutl life to eliminate violence against persons. The Kwakiutl statements on fighting with property give an accurate sketch of the nature and the timing and the main cause of the historical change that occurred in their culture following the first intensive contact with the new culture: "When I was young I have seen streams of blood shed in war. But since that time the white man came and stopped up that stream of blood with wealth."

Bibliography

Adam, L.

1922. "Potlatch. Eine ethnologisch-rechtswissenschaftliche Betrachtung." *Festschrift Eduard Seler*, Stuttgart, pp. 27–45.

Bascom, W.

1948. "Ponapean Prestige Economy." *Southwestern Journal of Anthropology*, Vol. 4, No. 2.

Barnett, H. G.

1938. "The Nature of the Potlatch." *American Anthropologist*, Vol. 40, pp. 349–358.

1939. "The Gulf of Georgia Salish." *University of California Anthropogical Records*, Vol. 1.

Benedict, Ruth

1934. *Patterns of Culture*, Boston, Houghton Mifflin.

Boas, Franz

1887. "Census and Reserves of the Kwakiutl Nation." *American Geographical Society*, Vol. 19, No. 3.

1888a. "The Development of the Culture of North America." *Science*, Vol.12.

1888b. "Gleanings from the Emmons Collection of Ethnological Specimens from Alaska," "Chinook Songs." *Journal of American Folk-Lore*, Vol. 1, No. 3.

1888c. "The Houses of the Kwakiutl Indians of British Columbia." *Proceedings of the U. S. National Museum*, Vol. 11.

1888d "Preliminary Notes on the Indians of British Columbia." *British Association for the Advancement of Science*, Vol. 58.

1889a. "First General Report on the Indians of British Columbia." *British Association for the Advancement of Science*, Vol. 59.

1889b. "The Indians of British Columbia." *Proceedings and Transactions of the Royal Society of Canada*, Series 1, Vol. 6, No. 2.

1889c. "Über seine Reisen in Britisch-Columbien." *Sonder-Abdruck aus den Verhandlungen der Gesellschaft für Erdkunde zu Berlin*, Vol. 6.

1891a. "Ein Besuch in Victoria auf Vancouver." *Globus*, Vol. 59.

1891b. "Reise an die pacifische Küste." *Aus den Verhandlungen der Berliner anthropologischen Gesellschaft*. Außerordentliche Sitzung am 14. Februar, 1891.

1893. "Vocabulary of the Kwakiutl Language." *Proceedings of the American Philosophical Society*, Vol. 31.

1894. "Classification of the Languages of the North Pacific Coast." *Memoirs of the International Congress of Anthropology*, Chicago, 1894.

1895. *Indianische Sagen von der Nordpacifischen Küste Amerikas*. Berlin.

1896a. "Die Entwicklung der Geheimbünde der Kwakiutl Indianer." *Festschrift Adolf Bastian*, Berlin.

1896b. "The Indians of British Columbia." *Journal of the American Geographical Society of New York*, Vol. 28, pp. 229–243.

1896c. "Songs of the Kwakiutl Indians." *International Archiv für Ethnographie*, Vol. 9, Supplement.

1897. "The Social Organization and the Secret Societies of the Kwakiutl Indians." *Report of the U.S. National Museum for 1895*, Washington.

1904. "Der Einfluß der sozialen Gliederung der Kwakiutl auf deren Kultur." *International Congress of Americanists*, Vol. 14, No. 1.
1905a. "Kwakiutl Texts." *Memoir of the American Museum of Natural History*, Vol. 5.
1905b. "Kwakiutl Texts, Second Series." *Memoir of the American Museum of Natural History*, Vol. 14.
1909. "The Kwakiutl of Vancouver Island." *Memoir of the American Museum of Natural History*, Vol. 8.
1910a. "Kwakiutl, An Illustrative Sketch. Extract from the Handbook of American Indian Languages." *Bureau of American Ethnology Bulletin*, No. 40, Pt. 1.
1910b. "Kwakiutl Tales." *Columbia University Contributions to Anthropology*, Vol. II.
1916. "Tsimshian Mythology." *Bureau of American Ethnology, Report*, No. 31.
1920. "The Social Organization of the Kwakiutl." *American Anthropologist*, Vol. 22, No. 2.
1921. "Ethnology of the Kwakiutl." Pts. I and II, *Bureau of American Ethnology Report*, No. 35.
1924a. "A Revised List of Kwakiutl Suffixes." *International Journal of Linguistics*, Vol. III.
1924b. "The Social Organization of the Tribes of the North Pacific Coast." *American Anthropologist*, Vol. 26, No. 3.
1924c. Lecture Notes. Barnard College.
1925. "Contributions to the Ethnology of the Kwakiutl." *Columbia University Contributions to Anthropology*, Vol. III.
1927a. "Die Ausdrücke für einige religiöse Begriffe der Kwakiutl-Indianer." *Festschrift Meinhof*, Hamburg.
1927b. *Primitive Art*. Oslo.
1930. "The Religion of the Kwakiutl Indians." Part I, Texts, Part II, Translations. *Columbia University Contributions to Anthropology*, Vol. X.
1932. "Current Beliefs of the Kwakiutl Indians." *Journal of American Folklore*, Vol. 45. No. 176.
1934. "Geographical Names of the Kwakiutl Indians." *Columbia University Contributions to Anthropology*, Vol. XX.
1935. "Kwakiutl Culture as Reflected in Mythology." *Memoir of the American Folklore Society*, No. 28.
1936. "Die Individualität primitiver Kulturen." *Reine und Angewandte Soziologie*, in honor of F. Tönnies, Leipzig.
1938. *General Anthropology*, Boston, D. C. Heath. F. Boas Ed. and Contributor.
1940. "Metaphorical Expression in the Language of the Kwakiutl Indians." *Race, Language and Culture*, New York.
1947. "Kwakiutl Grammar." *Transactions of the American Philosophical Society*, Vol. 37, Pt. 43, Philadelphia.
n. d. *Kwakiutl Ethnology*, MS.

BRABANT, REV. A. J.
1900. *Vancouver Island and its Missions.*

BUNZEL, RUTH
1938. "The Economic Organization of Primitive Peoples." Ch. VIII in *General Anthropology* ed. by Franz Boas.

BUSHNELL, DAVID I.
1928. "Drawings by John Webber of Natives of the Northwest Coast of America, 1778." *Smithsonian Miscellaneous Collections*, Vol. 80, No. 10.

COLLISON, W. H.
1915. *In the Wake of the War Canoe*. London.
COOK, CAPTAIN JAMES
1809. *The Voyages of Captain James Cook*, Vol. VI, Book Iv. London.
CROSBY, REV. THOMAS
1907. *Among the An-ko-me-nums or Flathead Indians of the Pacific Coast*. Toronto.
CURTIS, E. S.
1915. *The North American Indian*, Vo. X. *The Kwakiutl*, Vol. XI. Norwood.
CURTIS, NATALIE
1907. *The Indians' Book*. New York.
DAWSON, G. M.
1887. "Notes and Observations on the Kwakiool People of the Northern Part of Vancouver Island and Adjacent Coasts, made during the Summer of 1885; with a vocabulary of about seven hundred words." *Proceedings and Transactions of the Royal Society of Canada for the year 1887*, Vol. V, Section II, pp. 63–98.
1888. "Customs and Arts of the Kwakiool." *Popular Science Monthly*, No. 33, pp. 345–352.
DRUCKER, PAUL
1939. "Rank, Wealth and Kinship in Northwest Coast Society." *American Anthropologits*, Vol. 41, No. 1.
DUBOIS, CORA
1936. "The Wealth Concept as an Integrative Factor in Tolowa-Tututni Culture," in *Essays in Anthropology presented to A. L. Kroeber*, Berkley.
FORD, CLELLAN S.
1941. *Smoke from their Fires. The Life of a Kwakiutl Chief*. New Haven.
FRANCHÈRE, GABRIEL
1854. *Narrative of a Voyage to the Northwest Coast of America in the Years 1811, 1812, 1813 and 1814 or the First American Settlement on the Pacific*. J. V. Huntington, Translator. New York.
GARFIELD, VIOLA E.
1939. "Tsimshian Clan and Society." *University of Washington Publications in Anthropology*, Vol. 7, No. 3.
GIBBS, G.
1877. "Vocabulary of the Kwa'kiutl'." *Contributions to North American Ethnology*, Vol. I. Department of Interior. U.S.Geographical and Geological Survey of the Rocky Mountain Region.
GOLDMAN, IRVING
1937. "The Kwakiutl Indians of Vancouver Island," in *Cooperation and Competition among Primitive Peoples*. ed. by Margaret Mead, New York.
HALL, A. J.
1888. "A Grammar of the Kwakiutl Language." *Transactions of the Royal Society of Canada*, Vol. VI, Section II.
HAYWARD, V.
1918. "The Indians of Alert Bay." *Canadian Magazine*, Vol. LI.
HENSHAW, H. K.
1888. "Kwakiool Indians." *American Anthropologist*, o. s., No. 1.
HERSKOVITS, M. J.
1940. *Economic Life of Primitive Peoples*. New York.

HILL-TOUT, CHARLES
1907. *The Native Races of the British Empire. British North America I.* "The Far West the Home of the Salish and the D'e'n'e." London.

HOWAY, F. W.
1914. ed. "A New Vancouver Journal." *Washington Historical Quarterly,* Vol. V, No. 3.
1915a. ed. "A New Vancouver Journal." *Washington Historical Quarterly,* Vol. VI, No. 1.
1915b. "Some Remarks Upon the New Vancouver Journal." *Washington Historical Quarterly,* Vol. VI, No. 2.
1923. "Early Days of the Maritime Fur-Trade on the Northwest Coast." *Canadian Historical Review,* Vol. IV, No. 1.
1924. "The Early Literature of the Northwest Coast." *Proceedings and Transactions of the Royal Society of Canada,* Series 3, Vol. XVIII, No. ii.
1925. "Indian Attacks upon Maritime Traders of the North-west Coast." *Canadian Historical Review,* Vol. VI, No. 4.
1944. "William Sturgis: The Northwest Fur Trade." *The British Columbia Historical Quarterly,* Vol. VIII.

HOWAY, F. W., W. N. SAGE, and H. P. ANGUS
1942. *British Columbia and the United States.* Toronto.

HUNT, GEORGE
1906. "The Rival Chiefs". *Boas Anniversary Volume.* New York.

JACOBSEN, ADRIAN
1884. "*Reise an der Nordwestküste Amerikas 1881–1883.*" Leipzig, ed. A. Woldt.

JEWITT, JOHN R.
1931. *A Journal Kept at Nootka Sound by John R. Jewitt* one of the survivors of the crew of the Ship Boston during a captivity among the Indians from March, 1803 through July, 1805. Reprinted from the original edition. Boston.

KANE, PAUL
1859. *Wanderings of an Artist among the Indians of North America.* London.

KROEBER, A. L.
1917. "The tribes of the Pacific Coast of North America." *Proceedings of the 19th International Congress of Americanists.*
1923. "American Culture and the Northwest Coast." *American Anthropologist,* Vol. 25, No. 1.
1934. "Native American Population." *American Anthropologist,* Vol. 36, No. 1.

LENOIR, RAYMOND
1924. "Sur l'institution du potlatch." *Revue Philosophique,* Vol. XCVII.

LORD, JOHN KEAST
1866. *The Naturalist in Vancouver Island and British Columbia.* 2 Vols. London.

MACLEOD, WM. C.
1924. "Certain Aspects of the Social Organization of the Northwest Coast and of the Algonkian." *International Congress of Americanists,* Vol. XXI.
1927. "Some Social Aspects of Aboriginal American Slavery." *Journal de la Société des Americanists,* Vol. XIX.
1928a. *The American Indian Frontier.* New York.
1928b. "Economic Aspects of Indigenous American Slavery." *American Anthropologist,* Vol. 30, No. 4.

McIntyre, D. N.
1914. *The Fisheries in Canada and Its Provinces,* Vol. 21 The Pacific Province, Pt. II, in *Canada and Its Provinces* ed. by A. Shortt and A. G. Doughty. Toronto 1914.

Mayne, R. C.
1862. *Four Years in British Columbia and Vancouver Island.* London.

Mead, Margaret
1937. *Cooperation and Competition among Primitive Peoples.* New York.

Meares, John
1791. *Voyages made in the Years 1788 and 1789.* 2 Vols. London.

Moret, A., and G. Davy
1926. *From Tribe to Empire.* Translated by V. Gordon Childe, New York.

Murdock, George P.
1936. "Rank and Potlatch among the Haida." *Yale University Publications in Anthropology,* No. 13.

Newcombe, C. F., ed
1923. "Menzies Journal of Vancouvers' Voyage." *Archives of British Columbia,* Memoir No. V.

Niblack, A. P.
1888. "The Coast Indians of southern Alaska and northern British Columbia." *Report of the U. S. National Museum for 1888.*

Oppel, U.
1893. "Die Vermehrung der Weißen im britischen Nordamerika." *Globus,* Vol. 63.

Quimby, George I.
1948. "Culture Contact on the Northwest Coast, 1785–1795." *American Anthropologist,* Vol. 50, No. 2.

Read, Charles H.
1892. "An Account of a Collection of Ethnological Specimens formed during Vancouver's Voyage in the Pacific Ocean, 1790–1795." *Journal of the Royal Anthropological Institute of Great Britain and Ireland,* Vol. XXI.

Rich, E. E., ed.
1941. "The Letters of John McLoughlin From Fort Vancouver to the Governor and Committee. First Series, 1825–1838." *Champlain Society.* Toronto.
1943. "The Letters of John McLoughlin. Second Series, 1839–44." *The Champlain Society.* Toronto.

Rivera, Trinita
1949. "Diet of a Food-Gathering People, with Chemical Analysis of Salmon and Saskatoons." pp. 19ff. in *Indians of the Urban Northwest* ed. by Marian W. Smith.

Sage, Walter N.
1930. *Sir James Douglas and British Columbia.* Toronto.

Sapir, Edward
1914. "Indian Tribes of the Coast." Vol. XXI in *Canada and Its Provinces,* ed. by A. Shortt and A. G. Doughty. Toronto.
1915. "The Social Organization of the West Coast Tribes." *Proceedings and Transactions of the Royal Society of Canada.* Series 3, Vol. IX, No. ii.

Sapir, Edward, and M. Swadesh
1939. *Nootka Texts. Tales and Ethnological Narratives with Grammatical Notes and Lexical Materials.* Philadelphia.

Sheldon, Charles
1912. *The Wilderness of the North Pacific Coast Islands.* New York.

SHORTT, A. and A. G. DOUGHTY
1914. *Canada and Its Provinces.* 20 Vols. Vol. XX *The Pacific Province.* Pts. I and II. Toronto.

SMITH, MARIAN W.
1938. "The War-Complex of the Plains Indians." *Proceedings of the American Philosophical Society,* Vol. 78, No. 3.
1940. "The Puyallup-Nisqually." *Columbia University Contributions to Anthropology,* Vol. 32. New York.
1949. "Indians of the Urban Northwest." *Columbia University Contributions to Anthropology,* Vol. 36, New York.

STRONG, THOMAS N.
1930. *Cathlamet on the Columbia.* Oregon.

SWAN, JAMES G.
1857. *The Northwest Coast or Three Years Residence in Washington Territory.* New York.

SWADESH, M.
1948. "Motivations in Nootka Warfare." *Southwestern Journal of Anthropology,* Vol. 4, No. 1.

SWANTON, JOHN R.
1909. "The Haida." *Memoir of the American Museum of Natural History,* Jesup North Pacific Expedition, Vol. V, Pt. I.

THWAITES, R. G.
1904. *Early Western Travels.* Vol. VII *Ross's Adventures of the First Settlers on the Oregon or Columbia River, 1810–1813.* Cleveland.

TOLMIE, W. F., and G. M. DAWSON
1884. *Comparative Vocabularies of the Indian Tribes of British Columbia.* Montreal.

UNITED STATES FEDERAL TRADE COMMISSION
1919. *Report on Canned Foods.* Washington.

VANCOUVER, GEORGE
1798. *Voyage of Discovery to the North Pacific Ocean and round the World.* 3 Vols. London.

CANADIAN GOVERNMENT PUBLICATIONS
1872–1946 *Annual Report on Indian Affairs.* Ottawa.
Board of Inquiry into the Cost of Living in Canada 1915 *Report of the Board.* Ottawa.
Dominion of Canada Bureau of Statistics. *Canada Yearbook.*
1940. *Revised Statutes of Canada,* Vol. II.